THE DALAI LAMA'S CAT AND

THE ƒOUR ꓑAWS OF

SPIRITUAL
SUCCESS

ALSO BY DAVID MICHIE

FICTION

The Dalai Lama's Cat

The Dalai Lama's Cat and The Art of Purring

The Dalai Lama's Cat and The Power of Meow

The Queen's Corgi

The Magician of Lhasa

The Astral Traveler's Handbook & Other Tales

NONFICTION

Buddhism for Busy People: Finding Happiness in an Uncertain World

Hurry Up and Meditate: Your Starter Kit for Inner Peace and Better Health

Enlightenment to Go: Shantideva and the Power of Compassion to Transform Your Life

Mindfulness is Better than Chocolate

Buddhism for Pet Lovers: Supporting our Closest Companions through Life and Death

The Dalai Lama's Cat and

The Four Paws of
Spiritual
Success

DAVID MICHIE

CONCH
CONCH BOOKS

CONCH
Conch Books, an imprint of
Mosaic Reputation Management (Pty) Ltd

Cover design: Sue Campbell Book Design
Author photo: Janmarie Michie

Cataloguing-in-Publication details are available from the
National Library of Australia www.trove.nla.gov.au

ISBN 978 0 9944881 8 3 (Print USA version)
ISBN: 978 0 9944881 9 0 (Ebook USA version)

DEDICATION

With heartfelt gratitude to my precious gurus:
Les Sheehy, extraordinary source of inspiration and wisdom;
Geshe Acharya Thubten Loden, peerless master and
embodiment of the Dharma;
Zasep Tulku Rinpoche, precious Vajra Acharya and yogi.

Guru is Buddha, Guru is Dharma, Guru is Sangha,
Guru is the source of all happiness.
To all gurus I prostrate, go for refuge and make offerings.

May this book carry waves of inspiration from my own gurus
To the hearts and minds of countless living beings.

May all beings have happiness and the true causes of happiness.
May all beings be free from suffering and the true causes
of suffering;
May all beings never be parted from the happiness that is without
suffering, the great joy of nirvana liberation;
May all beings abide in peace and equanimity, their minds free
from attachment and aversion, and free from indifference.

PROLOGUE

ARE YOU CURIOUS, DEAR READER? IF YOU WERE TO FIND YOUR-self padding past an alcove concealed by a curtain, would your every instinct be to tug back the fabric—or, indeed, push under it—to see what lay behind?

Making your way down a familiar street, if you came to a door which, for your entire existence, had been closed, but today was ajar, would you pause to take a good, long peek inside? Or at the very least, steal a sideways glance? And if that door led to a mysterious corridor which, in turn, opened onto a secret courtyard, or perhaps a lamp-lit room filled with intriguing artifacts, might you be tempted to venture inside?

Oh, there's no need to reply. I already know your answer. That's something we have in common, you and I. You are not the kind of reader—and I am most certainly not the kind of cat—satisfied by mundane routine. We have inquiring minds, do we not? We ask questions. Discover things. Leave a newly emptied cardboard box in the middle of a room, and we will be the first to jump inside it.

And I'm not merely being literal. As you will also have assumed. Which is another thing we have in common, you and I—the wish to have **fun** while exploring possibilities of the greatest profundity. Why communicate on a single level, pray tell, when you can do so on two levels simultaneously? Where's the joy in that?

Of all the subjects about which we're curious, the one that makes our tails tingle and whiskers positively quiver is, of course, the one that concerns our ultimate purpose, our deepest wellbeing. What are our destinies, dear reader, and how may we affect them in this lifetime and whatever follows? Is it true that the nature of our mind is radiant, boundless and serene? If so, how do we go about experiencing this extraordinary reality?

There are different places a cat might seek out answers to such questions. One such venue, a place teeming with great wisdom, is The Himalaya Book Café, one of my favorite places in the world. A short distance down the road from Namgyal Monastery, where I live with His Holiness, the bookshelves of this delightful emporium offer a treasure trove of spiritual and esoteric reading. Among the many titles, you will discover global bestsellers along the lines of: *The Six Laws of This, The Seven Habits of That* or *The Eight Rules of The Other*.

Just looking at them puts me in the mood for a nap. How much effort would it take to plow through all those earnest volumes, I sometimes wonder? To try to remember all that they contain? Then to apply the laws, habits and rules to one's own life? Do people actually go through life constantly monitoring their activities against a checklist of items which grows in length every time a new such book is propelled onto the bookshelves?

It all seems very complicated. Unnecessarily so. Because day after day as I sit on the windowsill, listening to His Holiness offer wisdom to countless visitors, he is **never** complicated. Guests don't leave his office clutching life prescriptions itemizing six of these plus seven of those, like a bubble pack of multi-colored capsules to be ingested daily. On the contrary, the Dalai Lama's advice is usually very simple. And as a famous cat once said—it may even have been me—simplicity is the ultimate sophistication, is it not?

Rather than venturing down to The Himalaya Book Café and the latest batch of imports, if it's enlightenment one is after, then it's far better to stay at home. Sprawled in the dappled light of my delightful, first-floor sill, where I can keep an eye on the courtyard below and all the comings and goings at Namgyal Monastery. The perfect vantage point from which to maintain maximum surveillance with minimum effort.

For years I have sat in this same spot following the change of seasons outside, while eavesdropping on His Holiness' conversations within. For years I have been on the receiving end of compliments about the adorableness of my sapphire-blue eyes, my charcoal-colored face, the sumptuousness of my cream coat, and the delightful bushiness of my gray tail.

When the Dalai Lama rescued me from almost certain death, and I was a mere scrap of a kitten, everything in His Holiness' apartment was fresh and exciting. In those very early days I was confined to the first floor, a space quite big enough for a tiny, if inquisitive, being. Seven years have passed, and I have long since become thoroughly acquainted not only with

His Holiness' apartment, but also with every nook and cranny of Namgyal Monastery, not to mention all the most interesting neighborhood haunts. They are all now familiar territory.

Recently I came to realize that, without setting out to do so, I have become equally familiar with the conversations that go on within. During my earlier days, intrigued by every passing prince, president or pop star, the questions they came with were as new and unfamiliar to me as the Dalai Lama's apartment had been, when I was a tiny kitten.

Seven years on, I have come to realize that whatever questions they may ask His Holiness, the answers are always variations on the same themes.

However, instead of becoming bored with these teachings, the opposite is true: the more acquainted I become with them, the more deeply they touch me. Whenever I hear the Dalai Lama explain the value of loving kindness, in his distinctive bass voice, I find myself resonating with exactly those same qualities, as though by transmitting the idea, he makes them manifest. Whenever he throws back his head and laughs—which he does often—he simultaneously releases a joy within me, and whoever else is in the room, that is quite palpable. And whenever he explains the path to fulfillment and inner peace, I am struck with such a profound sense of wellbeing that I wish it could ripple out to every being possessing fur, feathers or fins—as well as those relative few on our planet who do not—so that we may all come to know our own true nature as a tangible, all-pervading truth.

And I have also come to understand another thing: the reason why so many people seek out the Dalai Lama isn't necessarily because of what he might say. It's because of the way he makes them **feel**. Words and insights may be important, because they suggest the reason for the way he is why he is. They point to how we, too, can cultivate those same qualities we find so attractive in him. Long after people have forgotten every last word that His Holiness has said, they still remember how he touched their heart. And they love him for it.

Often at the end of an audience with His Holiness, a visitor will ask if there's a book they should read to understand the Tibetan Buddhist path. The Dalai Lama may give them a copy of a recommended title—such as Shantideva's classic, *Guide to the Bodhisattva's Way of Life*. Alternatively, he may recommend another book, or ask one of his Executive Assistants to provide more details to the visitor on the way out.

Whether or not his guests ever get around to actually reading these books is an interesting point. For it seems as if, in asking for a book suggestion, they are requesting a keepsake. A souvenir. Something to keep alive the extraordinary flame lit by his presence.

One evening around five o'clock, His Holiness' two Executive Assistants came into his office for their daily review. As always, Oliver, the Englishman who worked as the Dalai Lama's translator, had poured three cups of green tea which they were enjoying. Tenzin, His Holiness' adviser on monastic matters and the quintessential diplomat, sat next to Oliver on the sofa facing their boss. I was sprawled out on my own armchair next to His Holiness.

"We gave your American visitor the book you requested," reported Tenzin. A famous talk show host had visited us earlier that afternoon.

The Dalai Lama looked pensive for a few moments, before shrugging. "A useful book. Perhaps he will read it. But for him, maybe, not ideal."

On the sofa, Oliver and Tenzin exchanged a significant glance. The matter of what book to offer visitors was one they had discussed many times over the years.

Oliver, being a Westerner, was often more forthright than the others in the Dalai Lama's circle. He leaned forward on the sofa, "Your Holiness, what would an ideal book look like?"

The Dalai Lama nodded as he pondered, before saying, "It must cover the key elements of the path." He used both hands to sweep a circle in front of him. He listed the themes with which I had become long familiar. I counted them. There were four.

"An introductory book?" queried Oliver.

His Holiness held up his right hand in a cautioning way. "But not simplistic." His eyes met Oliver's with a mischievous twinkle. "You Westerners are not quite the barbarians that we Tibetans thought you were back in the 1960s."

They all chuckled. When lamas first emerged from behind the Himalayas to go to Europe, USA and Australia, they had imagined that Westerners, steeped in their materialist ways, would have little interest in the subtleties of mind training, let alone exploring the true nature of their own consciousness.

What they'd found had astonished them.

"High level, but not dumbed down?" queried Oliver.

"And …" His Holiness continued, "the book should include explanations about the mystical things," he chuckled again.

"You mean like oracles?" asked Oliver with a grin. "Telepathy?"

I turned my head to tune in more closely.

The Dalai Lama nodded as he laughed.

"Astral traveling and the like?" continued Oliver.

I noticed that Tenzin was taking no part in the conversation. Still seated beside his fellow Executive Assistant, it was as though he had dissolved into the background, removed himself from the conversation by his reticence.

At this point His Holiness looked directly at Oliver and said, "As my translator on so many books already, perhaps you would like to write this one?"

In an instant I realized why Tenzin had been keeping so quiet.

Oliver began coughing, his pale face turning pink. "Your Holiness!" he spluttered.

"You are familiar with the main themes."

"Yes, but …" Oliver was gripped by another paroxysm of wheezing. For this man—a translator, no less—who usually had no difficulty giving voice to the most nuanced and complex matters, to be rendered speechless was most unusual.

As he was doubled up, gasping for air, the Dalai Lama glanced over at Tenzin with a playful twinkle. "You could think of a title that is …" he tried to think of the word.

"Catchy?" prompted Tenzin.

"Yes. Like in the airport bookshops."

Given his constant travels, these were places with which His Holiness was familiar. Glancing over at me, the Dalai Lama seemed to be reading my mind—and not for the first time. "The Six Rules of something!" he gripped the arm of his chair as he chortled.

Recovering from his coughing episode, Oliver realized he was being made fun of. Sort of. Though perhaps not entirely. He gave careful thought to what he was about to say. "The ideal book should explain the main themes of Tibetan Buddhism. And what people find magical—like rebirth and so forth. But that isn't enough."

The Dalai Lama raised his eyebrows.

"What people want, more than anything, isn't just your wisdom. It's the way you make them **feel**. We need to somehow communicate your presence."

In an instant I realized where clever Oliver was going with this. "I'm not sure I'm the right person to do that," he said.

His Holiness pondered for a moment before asking. "Then who is?"

Deciding we must be getting near dinnertime, I stirred on the armchair, stretching out all of my legs with a luxuriant quiver.

The timing of this maneuver, I have to confess, was as crass as Oliver's point had been subtle. Around the table, all three men laughed. "I think we have a volunteer," chuckled the Dalai Lama.

"And perhaps a catchy title?" suggested Oliver, gesturing towards my outstretched limbs. "The Four Paws of Spiritual Success!"

They all chuckled before His Holiness observed, "That's not such a bad title. After all, the Tibetan Buddhist path may be said to comprise four particular aspects. Four practices which are our challenge to embody." Gesturing towards a beautiful image of Shakyamuni Buddha hanging on his wall he murmured, "We are reminded of these four elements every time we see the representation of an enlightened being." Oliver and Tenzin nodded sagely.

I looked over at the wall-hanging. Reminded of four elements, I wondered? Were we?

Later that evening, I was perched on the bed, paws neatly tucked under me, while the Dalai Lama sat close by, meditating. This was one of my favorite times of the day, our room lit with the soft glow of a solitary lamp. His Holiness' powerful, yet gentle compassion pervaded outwards beyond this room, and even Namgyal Monastery, to encompass lands and realms of existence far beyond. As the focus of his meditation turned to loving kindness, I began to purr softly, continuing all the while until he finished his session.

That was when he reached out to stroke me. "They are right, my little Snow Lion," he said, using the very special name which only he ever called me. In Tibet, snow lions are a symbol of fearlessness, power and joy. "You are tuned in."

I purred even more loudly.

"You have listened to me for thousands of hours," he continued to massage my face with his fingernails, just the way I liked it. "You know the wisdom to be shared. Most of all," he leaned over, briefly whispering in my ear, "you know how to communicate loving kindness."

As my purr rose to a crescendo, I turned to meet his eyes directly—a privilege bestowed only rarely by we cats.

"If you can help make others feel this way," he touched his heart. "Wonderful!"

Which is how, dear reader, you come to be holding this book in your hands. As much from a wish to convey an energetic presence, a feeling, as the profound wisdom of the Dalai Lama.

But if I may let you into a secret at this early stage, the sense of oceanic wellbeing people so frequently feel in His Holiness' presence isn't actually coming from him. He is an enabler, if you will, a facilitator. He is so pure of heart and so utterly free from ego, that what he does is reflect back to those he is with their own, ultimate nature. Their highest version of themselves.

If you're wondering how the presence of an enlightened being, a bodhisattva, may be communicated on the pages of a book written by a flawed and complex—if extremely beautiful—cat, let me confess that my only job here is to offer you a mirror. A looking glass of a particular kind. One that reflects back not the contours of your nose or the arch of your brow, but which provides a much deeper reflection of who and what you are. One which penetrates beneath the surface persona with whom you are no doubt all too familiar, to the truth of the consciousness abiding within.

This is a reflection with which you may be unfamiliar. One which may even catch you unawares. Look closely—there's no need to be afraid. What you will discover, if you ever doubted it, is that your own true nature is quite different from whatever blemishes and imperfections may temporarily obscure it. Self-criticism may drive you to focus on your own failings so much that you appear profoundly tainted; but the simple truth is that whatever abides in your mind is only ever temporary. Fleeting. Your consciousness can never be permanently contaminated, no more than water can be.

As we will explore in the pages that follow, the delightful truth is that the enduring qualities of your mind may be quite different from what you might suppose. Your consciousness is, in reality, both boundless and radiant, allowing any thought or sensation to arise, abide and pass. Once you penetrate beneath whatever surface turmoil may sometimes exist, your mind has the quality of tranquility that is, in fact, oceanic.

And if these statements seem as extravagant as my own sumptuous fur coat, let me add just one final observation, dear reader. At heart, you are a being whose pristine nature is nothing other than pure, great love and pure, great compassion. Mine too!

CHAPTER ONE

I COULD HARDLY BELIEVE MY OWN EYES! SITTING BENEATH MR Patel's market stall at the gates to Namgyal Monastery, the same place I had once observed him from my first-floor windowsill, was the most magnificent, mackerel-striped tabby in Dharamshala.

Could it really be him? Mambo, the father of my kittens? The gorgeous, muscular beast who had appeared in my life when I was still an impressionable young feline-about-town—before, just as enigmatically, vanishing?

My paw steps quickened, which required no small effort. The street outside The Himalaya Book Café, where I had spent the afternoon, had quite a slope to it. I was no longer in the prime of youth. And my rear legs hurt more than ever.

From the time I was tiny when I had been dropped onto the pavement, I had suffered from wonky back legs. Legs which had always felt awkward, and lately had even begun to burn.

Pushing through the pain, I made my way towards the gates as quickly as I could. With monks coming and going through the entrance, and market stalls plying their trade directly outside, a cat could easily slip out of sight in the general tumult. Especially one as well camouflaged as a tabby.

I hurried ever faster, ducking behind the row of stalls. I headed towards Mr. Patel's stall, the last in the row. Scanning through the moving legs and robes and saris, I tried to keep track of the unexpected visitor.

But he was no longer there. Nor on the nearby tree trunk, where he used to climb. I paused, surveying the area, wondering where to go next.

Suddenly, from behind a garbage bin, just a few feet to my right, I heard a low-pitched yowl. It was filled with menace. Instantly, my fur stood on end. Spinning round, almost losing balance, I was confronted by a ferocious tabby. Most definitely not Mambo. Savage of face and fur bristling, he was pure aggression.

I bared my fangs. He unleashed another, even louder, bloodcurdling warning before leaping forward. He was now only inches away. Well within striking range.

Instinct took over. I raised my right paw and snarled back. People were turning from Mr Patel's stall, voices raised in alarm.

The interloper, demanding dominance, fixed me with a gaze of total hatred. Young and lithe, no doubt he believed he could beat me in any fight.

But I wasn't giving way. I had been pursued in the past. I'd learnt not to run at the first sign of threat. My resistance only seemed to provoke him further. Incandescent with rage, he lashed at my head, huge claws extended.

People were screaming. And next thing there was a crash! A feeling of cold wetness. Human legs pushing between me and the tabby. Someone had thrown a pot of water at us. In the moments afterwards, I was scooped up and taken inside the gates of Namgyal before being set down in the courtyard. I glanced round, to see the tabby being shoved forcefully away.

There are some advantages to being recognized as the Dalai Lama's Cat.

With as much dignity as I could muster, given my soaking coat and shaken state, I returned across the courtyard to our building. The pain in all four paws was now so acute that it felt like I was walking on hot coals.

I skirted the building to the ground-floor window that was left open as my private entrance. Once inside, I stopped to groom myself. The water that had been thrown at us had been used to boil somebody's lunchtime rice. It was sticky and starchy, and tasted disgusting. Lifting a paw to my face, I felt a rawness where the intruder had clawed me—thankfully, my thick coat had protected me from worse damage.

Some minutes later, I made my way upstairs to the apartment I shared with His Holiness. On a normal day, it was bursting with warmth and kindness. But today the rooms were silent and in semi-darkness. The Dalai Lama was away traveling. It would be some days before he returned home.

I sat on the sill that evening, watching twilight fall over the Namgyal courtyard, looking across at the green light that

3

burned at the end of Mr. Patel's market stall, and I felt very, very sorry for myself indeed.

His Holiness arrived home several days later, and life instantly resumed its usual brisk pace. Arriving home late morning, the Dalai Lama barely had time to greet me before Oliver was in his office, ready to brief him on the guests who'd be arriving for lunch in less than an hour.

The subject of that day's gathering was 'Dharma in the Digital Age', a topic of some fascination if you didn't have more pressing things to worry about. Which I most certainly did.

For starters, that most unpleasant ambush by the tabby cat still had me badly rattled—I had never been threatened by another cat before. Namgyal Monastery had been largely feline-free, and therefore my private domain, for as long as I'd lived here. Having another cat show up and act like it was his territory was a most unwelcome development.

Of more immediate concern were the stabbing pains I felt whenever I walked. They had started, ominously, the day of the tabby ambush. And as each day passed, they seemed to get worse. Visits to The Himalaya Book Café had become so excruciating that I'd even begun to question whether a visit for my favorite *sole meunière* could be justified, given the torment inflicted every step of the way. Just going up and down the stairs to our apartment was a harrowing exercise.

But I never had a moment's doubt that once His Holiness returned, things would get better. Exactly how, I had no idea.

But I needed some quality time with the Dalai Lama. Just the two of us together.

The mood in the Dalai Lama's dining room that lunchtime was the same as it always was when he entertained visitors, his guests instantly responding to his lightness and spontaneity, his capacity to inspire their own benevolence. Social media gurus, contemplative neuroscientists, lamas and psychologists exchanged ideas, while savoring a delicious meal prepared in the kitchen downstairs by the two women who had become institutions in His Holiness' household—the voluble and larg-er-than-life VIP chef, Mrs. Trinci, and her beautiful daughter, Serena.

Apart from the Dalai Lama, my biggest fan at Namgyal from my earliest days had been Mrs Trinci. Italian, operatic, her arms clanking with gold bracelets, she had showered me with delectable culinary treats, pronouncing me to be The Most Beautiful Creature That Ever Lived, a title to which many oth-ers would be added in due course—not all of them quite so delightful.

Following a heart attack, and on her specialist's advice, Mrs. Trinci had come to the Dalai Lama for personal meditation lessons, over time becoming a mellower and less frenetic version of her former self—though no less a big-hearted one. When her daughter, Serena, had arrived back in Dharamshala after years working in some of Europe's most famous restaurants, Mrs. Trinci had begun to share the burden of her work as His Holiness' Executive Chef. Little did I know that, once drawn into Serena's world, the most intriguing revelations of my life would be uncovered.

Elegant and graceful, long dark hair sweeping straight down her back, since the moment I first caught sight of Serena, I'd been captivated by her compassionate energy. As well as helping her mother take care of the Dalai Lama's VIP guests, she had become co-manager of The Himalaya Book Café, along with its owner, Franc. We had instantly become firm friends and, from a variety of shelves, nooks and gateposts, I had witnessed the blossoming of her romance with the handsome and luminously intelligent Indian businessman she had met at yoga class—a man whose natural modesty concealed the fact that he just happened to be the Maharajah of Himachal Pradesh.

Serena had moved in with Sid—short for Siddhartha—once he had renovated a sprawling, colonial, mountainside home for them. Their home just happened to be a short walk away from my windowsill at Namgyal Monastery.

In time, I became aware of a strong connection to Sid; also to Zahra, his seventeen-year-old daughter—Sid's first wife having died in a car accident many years before. Zahra lived away from home at boarding school, returning home for holidays. From the very first time I'd caught sight of Zahra I had adored her, and I loved spending time at their home.

As was the case at all lunchtime meetings with the Dalai Lama, my own needs were not overlooked. Head Waiter Kusali brought a ramekin to where I sat on the sill. Today's meal was a casserole with the most deliciously thick gravy. As I lapped it up with noisy relish, several Silicon Valley executives glanced my way with expressions of amusement. During the meal, His

Holiness looked at me several times too, but with a different expression. Even though we had spent almost no time together alone since his return, he seemed to sense that all was not well in my world.

Finishing my meal, I washed my face—even grooming had become difficult with such painful paws—and settled down, waiting for the gathering to come to an end. I felt a bit better with a tummy full of Mrs. Trinci's delicious food.

But I still longed for the moment when I would have the Dalai Lama to myself.

Finally the guests were leaving, Tenzin and Oliver ushering them out of the room. His Holiness had already asked Dawa to pass on his compliments to the chefs, and to invite them upstairs so he could thank them personally, in what had become a delightful tradition. No sooner had the guests left than Dawa returned with a message.

"Mrs. Trinci has already left, Your Holiness," he announced.

"And Serena?"

"She says she was only helping her mother, so can't claim any credit for the meal. And she knows you've been away for a long time so is sure you must be very busy."

The Dalai Lama nodded. It was by no means the first time an invitation to say 'thank you' had been rebuffed, even if in the most diplomatic way. For some time His Holiness remained in his seat with a thoughtful expression—was he perceiving something that eluded me?—before looking directly at me. Getting up he said, "I think we should go to see her, don't you Snow Lion?"

As he made his way to the door, I hopped down from where I'd been sitting, bracing myself for the inevitable pain of landing. We walked through the apartment and into the corridor that led past the Executive Assistants' office. I tried my best to tread normally, even though each step was more painful than ever. Walking on my back paws, in particular, was pure torture.

We headed down the stairs and along a short passage to the VIP kitchen. His Holiness paused in the doorway, watching as Serena busied herself in the kitchen. Today's meal may have been over, but another was planned for a private visit by the Aga Khan in three days hence, which was the cause of much activity. Serena was opening cupboards, checking their contents, referring to a list, writing down items that needed to be stocked and going through the deep shelves of the fridge. She was so preoccupied that it was a while before she looked up and discovered she was not alone.

"Oh! Your Holiness!" As she folded her palms together at her heart, she flushed.

"My dear Serena!" The Dalai Lama walked over and gave her a hug. Glancing down, she saw me at his feet.

"And I see little Rinpoche came downstairs too," she observed as they broke apart.

"The meal was wonderful!" The Dalai Lama gazed at her closely.

"Thank you."

"Especially the main course."

"Vegetarian stroganoff. It's the gravy that makes it."

Long hair tucked under a chef's hat and not wearing any make-up, this Serena looked very different from the one who worked front of house at The Himalaya Book Café, or who ran her spice pack business from the office above the café. But more than that, today there seemed to be a tension in her face, a concern clouding her eyes.

"I am never too busy to see you," said the Dalai Lama. "But perhaps you are too busy to see me?" There was humor in his expression, but also concern.

His Holiness had known Serena since she was a little girl. Mrs. Trinci, who had been widowed at an early age, had brought her in to do her homework at the kitchen bench, while she got on with meal preparation. In those early days, way before my time, I'd been told how Serena was drawn to the Dalai Lama, so that he'd become like a father figure to her.

She may have spent over ten years in Europe, making her own way in the world, but when she'd returned to Dharamshala, her bond with His Holiness had been as strong as ever. They were like family, and he knew her every expression, which was why she had to break away from his gaze.

"I'm sorry, Your Holiness," she said. "I didn't mean to cause offence."

He shrugged indicating that this wasn't the point.

Looking back at her list and to the cupboards she admitted, "I **am** pretty stressed at the moment."

"The Aga Khan lunch?" queried the Dalai Lama.

Serena brushed away the suggestion. "No. Nothing to do with that." Swiveling away, she looked round the kitchen, everywhere except at him. Then chewing at her lip, she said somewhat reluctantly, "It's the business."

"Very busy?" His Holiness' tone was sympathetic.

"Not busy enough." She shot him a glance. "As you know, we did a roaring trade when we first started out. We doubled in size each year for the first three years. But we've hit a wall."

The spice pack idea had come about when tourists asked about the delicious sauces, marinades and seasonings which made their meals at The Himalaya Book Café so utterly irresistible. Consulting with the café's resident chefs, Nepalese brothers Jigme and Ngawang Dragpa, Serena had devised ways to package spice blends that could be delivered globally by mail order. When Sid had opened doors to local spice producers at wholesale prices, suddenly they were in business.

Beautiful branding and an efficient delivery service soon had The Himalaya Book Café Spice Packs heading out to the four corners of the world. And after Sid and Serena were married two years ago, they decided that all profits from the business should be used to support local youngsters get the training they needed to find work.

"You are worried for the children?" the Dalai Lama queried.

"There are so many of them!" Serena's voice rose. "And they've come to depend on us. We're their last chance!"

In a moment she had become as impassioned as Mrs. Trinci herself—a resemblance I'd seldom witnessed before.

"And the sales ..."

"Nosedived!" she was emphatic. "Back to where they were twelve months ago. Eighteen, even!" Unable to stand still a moment longer, she strode to the other side of the kitchen to collect her handbag. Unnecessarily. Before bringing it back and dumping it beside her list with a thud.

"It's not just one thing that's affecting our business, it's so many," her dark eyes blazed. "It's consumer fatigue. And massive competition. We're being regulated out of business in some markets. Only last week this new biosecurity law came in and we lost all our customers in Australia." She flicked both hands open, palms facing upwards. "Overnight!"

I looked up at the Dalai Lama. This was not the Serena I thought I knew. I had never seen my friend—whose name had always seemed so appropriate—in such a state. As I observed His Holiness, I sensed that he understood much more about what was happening. And for the first time I had an inkling that perhaps there was a deeper cause for Serena's frustration. That what she was talking about was only a proxy, a substitute for another cause of anguish.

"All the while …" she was gesturing outside, "our waiting list for kids needing basic IT skills just keeps getting longer and longer!"

Jaw tense, with a vein standing out on her neck, she seemed at the end of her tether. "I look at their little faces and I know how much they need my help, but I just don't seem able to turn things around!" She raised her hands to her head. "We've tried everything that might make a difference! You think something's going to work. Other people swear by doing this thing or that thing. You build up your hopes because you so desperately want it to come right …"

11

Suddenly she seemed to crumple, her shoulders slumping. Her eyes welled with tears. She turned to face the Dalai Lama, her face a portrait of misery. "I just feel like I'm failing everyone," she said.

His Holiness didn't say anything for a moment, simply stood and enveloped her in his benevolent attention.

"Sid especially," she said softly, glancing towards me with the warm-eyed glow of maternal feeling, which I was more familiar with.

Suddenly I understood what I sensed His Holiness already had. And it was as if, in that moment, a shift occurred in the room, so that we all knew what was really being discussed without the need for it to be made explicit. The deeper cause of Serena's torment.

When Serena had married Sid they'd made no secret of their wish to have a family together as soon as possible. Many of their friends had expected an announcement of that kind to follow within months. Two years later, none had been made.

"You have spoken to Sid?" asked the Dalai Lama softly.

"We talk about it all the time."

"He doesn't feel you're … letting him down?"

She shook her head miserably. "You know Sid. He'd never say that. He's too much the gentleman."

The Dalai Lama took one of her hands in his with the utmost gentleness. "Often, our greatest suffering is self-inflicted."

"**Self**-inflicted?" Her eyes widened.

"Perhaps because of attachment."

12

Serena's expression turned to one of hurt. "It's not like I'm desperate for a Maserati!"

"No, no," His Holiness shook his head. "Material things are only one source of attachment. A more frequent cause is attachment to outcomes."

"Outcomes?"

"To having things the way we want them."

"What if it's not just about me?" she objected, pulling her hand quickly out of his. "What if it's **other** people I'm concerned about?"

"This is not a moral judgment …" he tried to reassure her.

"Sounds like it to me!" she snapped. "Sounds very much like a judgment!"

Striding over to the counter, she grabbed the list she'd been making and threw it in her handbag. Tugging off her chef's hat, she tossed it towards the sink.

"You know, this is exactly the kind of conversation I didn't want to have …" she told him, eyes blazing. "It's why I didn't come upstairs. I don't need to be told that it's all in my mind. That if I change the way I think, then everything will be hunky-dory. Sometimes life is just shit—and that's all there is to it!"

With that, she strode out of the kitchen, grabbing the door as she left and slamming it behind her.

I stared at the door, shaken by what I had just witnessed. In the seven years I've lived with the Dalai Lama, no-one had ever stormed out of his presence, much less banged the door as they left. And the very last person in the world I would have thought would do so was serene Serena.

13

His Holiness reached down to stroke my neck. "Such suffering," he observed, softly. "May she soon be free of anger and attachment."

That afternoon, the Dalai Lama was officiating at the ordination of monks across the courtyard at the temple. I remained on my sill, dozing and waiting for the moment when I'd **finally** have some time alone with him. And as I waited, the kitchen scene replayed in my mind: Serena's misery. His Holiness' attempt to help. Her raised voice and the slammed door.

Anger and attachment, the two things he had wished her to be free of, were considered delusions in Tibetan Buddhism—a delusion being any mental factor that disturbs one's peace of mind. Both were said to arise from the same underlying cause: the belief that things, people or situations possess inherent qualities which make them desirable—in which case we want them; or undesirable—in which case we do not. I had sat through countless hours of the Dalai Lama explaining these basic principles to people. And Serena was as familiar with them as anyone.

When it came to applying them to everyday life, however, things weren't always so clear cut. Serena's peace of mind was disturbed—of that, there was no dispute. But what if her unhappiness hadn't been caused by thinking about herself? Instead of being self-inflicted, what about pain arising from concern for others? What did Buddhism have to say about that?

What's more, wasn't the wish to have a baby not an entirely natural, feminine instinct for many, something which flowed deeper than thought or concept? What if, on this occasion, His Holiness had got it wrong?

As it happened, I didn't have long to wait to learn the answer. As dusk fell over the Namgyal courtyard, His Holiness returned home. Tenzin came to switch on the lamps in our apartment and had gone to fetch His Holiness a cup of green tea, when there was a familiar knock on the door. We both looked up.

"I'm so, so sorry!" It was Serena, ashen-faced and tearful. "I don't know what came over me!"

Stepping over from the other side of the room, His Holiness gestured towards her and began to chuckle. "You!" Then he pointed at his door and acted out slamming it. "Boom!"

Shaking her head, she looked bereft. "Can you ever forgive me?"

He opened his arms and she came towards him. As they embraced she began to say, "I just want you to know ..."

"Yes, yes." He interrupted, patting her back. "Words are not necessary."

A short while later, Tenzin had brought them both tea and they were seated, facing each other across a table. "I know you said it's attachment that's causing me pain," began Serena.

The Dalai Lama looked at her quite sternly. "No judgment," he said.

"I'm just wanting to understand." She paused, trying to order her thoughts. "I really do want to help others—like these kids who need training. And I'm doing all I can to make the business work for them. So how is it possible **not** to be attached?"

His Holiness smiled before saying simply, "By understanding that your peace of mind, your wellbeing, does not depend on it."

She absorbed this in silence, before tilting her head. "That just sounds a bit cold. Lacking in compassion."

The Dalai Lama raised his eyebrows. "Compassion is the wish to relieve beings of suffering."

"Yes."

"Are we better able to help others when our minds are calm and ordered, or when there is great turmoil?" His hand motioned the rising and falling of waves.

Serena inclined her head.

"For the sake of self and others, if we wish to practice effective compassion, we need a calm mind," he said. "This is essential. What's more, non-attachment is in accordance with the truth."

Leaning forward in his seat, he studied her closely for a while. "I remember a time, you had just come back from Europe."

Serena smiled.

"You were home in Dharamshala. No job. No—what do you say—boyfriend?" he chuckled.

"One of the happiest times of my life!" she volunteered.

"Very happy, even though you weren't helping any children get computer skills."

She was shaking her head. "I hadn't thought of any of that back then."

"You see. No outcome. But still, very happy. The two," he held his hands palms facing upwards, some distance from each other, "have no relationship. Only when we **invent** a relationship, there is a problem. When we say, "I can only be happy when this happens" or "I can only feel peaceful if that happens," that's when we make a problem for ourselves.

"Attachment is when we believe that a person, a thing or an outcome is **necessary** for our happiness. At that moment, we turn the person, thing or outcome into a source of future suffering. We risk becoming enslaved to it. Much better to think: I am **already** the possessor of happiness and inner peace. To have this person, thing or outcome in my life—how wonderful! But it is not necessary for my fundamental wellbeing."

Serena was nodding slowly.

"And I will tell you the secret gift of non-attachment," the Dalai Lama's eyes sparkled. "When we are able to hold an outcome in our heart with genuine non-attachment, then it is much more likely to happen. Clinging with attachment not only causes misery. It also makes us less successful."

Following his every word closely, Serena asked him, "Even when it comes to falling pregnant?"

"Of course!" The Dalai Lama nodded, as though this was a statement of the obvious. "For you at the moment, too much stress."

"I have found myself worrying a lot lately. So many horrible things have happened, all in a short space of time."

"Then it is time for renunciation," announced His Holiness, "time to turn away from the **true** causes of your unhappiness."

"Which are not the spice pack problems. Or ... this" she touched her abdomen. "But attachment to how I'd like things to be?"

"Exactly. Renunciation is when you decide you've had enough. When you finally recognize that your unhappiness isn't coming from out there, but from your own mind. From battling the way that things are, and wishing them to be different. Renunciation is when we turn away from the suffering we are experiencing because of our attachment to the way we think that things should be, or perhaps bitterness about the way they are. You could say that renunciation is the start of our inner journey. Instead of fixating on external circumstances, we look within."

"In my heart I think I've known that I needed to let go."

"Let go. Let go," agreed His Holiness. "The more we let go, the more peace here." He touched his heart.

Serena regarded the Dalai Lama with an expression of gratitude. Then she stood up. "Now, I should let go of you. I've already taken up too much of your time today." Glancing towards the sill, she saw me lying on my side, watching them. "I'm sure you'll be wanting some quality time with little Rinpoche," she said.

As His Holiness rose from his chair, Serena stepped over to stroke me. Responding, I reached out both arms and legs, intending a full, tremulous, tummy stretch. But as I extended, my front, right claw caught on her wedding ring. Searing pain jolted through my whole side. I recoiled in agony.

"Rinpoche!" Serena was aghast, as I let out a yowl.

Bending, she studied my paw closely. At the same time, the Dalai Lama leaned over me too. Both caught sight of the same thing at the same time. His Holiness' eyebrows shot up in alarm. Serena's forehead furrowed in concern. "Oh, you poor little thing!" she wailed. She turned to the Dalai Lama, "Look at the length of them."

He was shaking his head. "I thought the way she was walking this afternoon was not quite right."

"All these weeks you've been away, and nobody looking out for her."

"We must take action." His Holiness' expression was serious. "Immediately."

I, dear reader, am not a cat who takes kindly to being held fast while having her claws trimmed. Even when the person doing the holding is the Dalai Lama, and the person doing the trimming is the Maharani of Himachal Pradesh. But no matter how much I writhed and wriggled, there was no escaping His Holiness' clutches. No evading the stainless steel blades of Serena's trimmers. One by one they worked their way round each of my paws until every last nail had been pruned.

As soon as they put me down, I stormed towards the Dalai Lama's desk as fast as my gray boots would take me, ears firmly pressed back. The desk was my place of safety. Under it, I was inaccessible to a human arm. Even as I made my way over, however, I became aware of something: the pain in my paws and legs had gone. Completely. There wasn't so much as the merest twinge of discomfort.

I inspected my paws by licking them. As I did, I realized that, bit by bit, I must have become used to my nails protruding. They had grown a little, then a little more, and I had become so accustomed to them being the way they were that I'd ignored them.

Serena was returning the trimmers to her handbag and preparing to go. "The greatest suffering is self-inflicted. Isn't that what you were saying this morning?" her tone was wry. "And even when you try to help ..."

Peering up between the legs of the desk, I saw His Holiness pretending to be me, lashing out one of his arms, fingers outstretched. Before segueing to a door slam. "Bang!" he laughed. "Same, same."

Surely not! I was indignant. You couldn't possibly equate the two. Could you?!

"Is it possible to become attached to attachment?" Serena asked, hitching her bag over her shoulder.

"Oh yes," said the Dalai Lama. "Sometimes the things we cling to most tightly are those that hurt us more than anything. But we keep on clinging because we don't believe there's a different way." Turning pensive, he murmured, "This is the great sadness of samsara. A person can be starving in a room, even though just along the passage, there is a kitchen with all the food she could possibly eat. But she has to walk to the kitchen by herself. She has to believe that it's there. There must come a time when she says, "Enough suffering, already! I must try something different.""

There is a particular ritual with which His Holiness and I sometimes end the day. Before retiring to bed, he will go into his own small kitchen, furnished with just a few culinary essentials. There he will put a slice of bread into a toaster, before switching on the kettle to make himself a cup of tea.

If I haven't already followed him, the aroma of toasting bread immediately summons me from wherever I am to sit at his feet, expectantly. Once toast is made—entirely for my delectation, as the Dalai Lama doesn't eat in the evening—he will cut a small corner for me and coat it liberally with butter, before putting it on a saucer and placing it before me.

The two of us enjoy our time together, His Holiness sitting at a small table sipping tea, while I crunch my buttered toast with relish.

"I am sorry I haven't been here for you, my little one," he said tonight, once I'd finished my toast and looked up at him. "Your claws grew so long."

He gazed at me thoughtfully, as I licked my right, front paw, relishing the way my tongue had free access to my velvet pads.

"We humans also have to be vigilant, just like you," he observed, as I began washing my face. "Our thoughts are like claws. They can be very helpful when we turn our mind to things. Develop ideas. Set goals. Express emotions. But if we aren't careful, these same thoughts can turn in on us and become the source of our greatest pain. They no longer help us take purposeful action, but instead are the cause of self-inflicted misery. Cat or human, we are the same."

Reaching down, he lifted me onto his lap, took my front, left paw in his hand and turned it sideways, gazing closely at my newly trimmed nails. "When we've had enough suffering and want to make a new start, that's renunciation," he said.

I fixed him with a sapphire-blue gaze of great devotion.

He leaned down to touch me with his cheek, murmuring softly, "You might say this is the first law—the first paw—of spiritual success. What do you think, little Snow Lion?"

When he put me back down on the floor I was struck by one of those bolts of energetic mania to which we cats are occasionally prone, especially after eating a scrumptious morsel. Even more so when feeling celebratory.

I hunched forwards. Shot a glance at him over my shoulder. Then bolted out of the kitchen, tearing down the corridor as fast as my fluffy gray boots would take me. It had been many weeks since I'd even thought of doing such a thing. And as I flew along the runner I was wonderfully liberated. Unburdened. Pain-free.

If this was how renunciation felt, how wonderful! I only wish I'd experienced the first paw of spiritual success a whole lot sooner!

At the door to the kitchen behind me, the Dalai Lama burst out laughing.

CHAPTER TWO

ARE YOU AN EXTRAORDINARY BEING, DEAR READER? DO YOU possess unusually acute powers of perception? Lucid insights into the minds of others? Is it the case that you often find yourself observing karma playing out in the lives of those around you, with the unwavering omniscience of a cat watching some drama unfold in the courtyard below, while perched on a sill high above?

If you are shaking your head, convinced that you have no such abilities, do you believe that you could, perhaps, develop them?

These may seem intrusive questions. Notions that make you ill at ease. Sadly, it is the lot of many beings to underrate themselves and undervalue their potential. To go through life with tragically diminished estimations of how capable they are.

If you do not already know this, you will soon discover
that I, for one, am not a cat who suffers from low self-esteem.
I see no point in false modesty, or pretending to be anything
other than sumptuously beautiful, irresistibly charming, or to
put it quite simply, the most popular being in the whole of
Dharamshala—bar one.

But not even I was aware of just how remarkable I am.
Much less my spectacular potential. A potential which, believe
it or not dear reader, you share with me in equal measure.

It required a particular chain of events for me to become
aware of all of this, beginning in the small hours of an unex-
ceptional Tuesday night.

You have no doubt heard the old adage: *Early to bed, early
to rise*? Well, the Dalai Lama is someone who takes this idea
very much to heart. Not only is he asleep at an hour when most
other people would just be sitting down to dinner, he also rises
at 3am—a time when the world is at its most serene. For the
next five hours, he meditates.

This nocturnal rhythm suits me perfectly, although I
wouldn't pretend to be his constant meditation partner. There
are times when I might make my way through the darkness
to my favorite windowsill, and from there look out across my
much-loved courtyard, turned magical by the ethereal starlight.
Or I may visit the kitchen for an urgently needed mouthful of
biscuits. Or simply curl up on the rug next to His Holiness and
accompany his whispered mantra recitation with an appreciative purr.

That particular Tuesday night, or to be more precise,
Wednesday morning, we were still fast asleep when I was

woken to the sound of shrieking. A squeal so piercing that for a moment I wondered if I had been dreaming. Jolting my head up I paused, absorbing the quiet of the night. For a few moments, there was only the undisturbed peace of the early hours.

Then it came again. From inside the building! I leapt up, making my way out of the bedroom as fast as my somewhat wonky rear legs would let me.

I recognized that sound. It triggered my most basic instincts. As I hurried to the door of His Holiness' apartment, the initial shrieks were joined by other electrifying voices. Just as I thought they would be.

From compulsion as much as anything, I reached out with my paw and scratched the apartment door. I thought it would be pointless, but worth trying. During the day, if the door was closed, there was always someone around to open it. But this was the middle of the night and the whole place was firmly locked up.

Raising my head, I sniffed at the air. Was it my imagination, or was the repulsive presence so strong that I could smell them even from here? There were more and more urgent squeals. And I knew exactly what was happening. A rat had made its way into the kitchen and found something. I had woken at the very moment it had signaled its discovery. Now others were piling in. Within minutes, there would be a feeding frenzy downstairs!

There was nothing for it. I headed back to the bedroom and jumped directly onto the sleeping form of the Dalai Lama. He reacted, trying to brush me off his chest. But I stepped over his arm, moving about on his rib cage and prodding him insistently through the sheet and blanket. I stretched out a paw and tapped him on the cheek. Gently, to begin with. Then insistently.

When all this failed to have the desired effect, I meowed in his face imploringly. **That** got him moving! In moments he was sitting up, "What's wrong, little Snow Lion?"

What's wrong?! Was he deaf? I may have meowed only a few inches from his ear, but how could he have slept through the cacophony going on in the kitchen.

I jumped off his bed and headed to the door. I threw a glance over my shoulder to make sure he was following. Together we headed through the apartment to the front door. The shrieking downstairs had reached delirious heights. How many of them could there be down there? And exactly what were they destroying?

Deciding that this was no time for ambiguity, as soon as I reached the front door, I started scratching at it.

"Oh, no, little one. Not now. It's the middle of the night." Exactly! And for the first time ever since I'd been living here, rats were on the rampage.

Whether His Holiness was still half asleep or chose to ignore what was happening, I didn't know. But as I continued scratching, I found myself being lifted away from the door. Carried through the apartment. Taken to a small laundry room and placed carefully on a litter tray.

"There," said the Dalai Lama. "No need to go out." And he returned to bed.

I went back immediately to the front door. I prowled and scratched and slashed my tail. For a while I crouched, inhaling the current of air passing through the narrow gap under the door, taking in the pungent aroma of the invaders—helpless to do anything about them.

I was outraged and frustrated. But more than anything, I was mystified. It seemed that His Holiness was completely unconcerned that his home was being invaded by a plague of rats. He acted like he couldn't care less!

The next day, when there came the inevitable report that rodents had found their way through an open window into the downstairs pantry, ruining bags of sugar, nuts and fresh fruit, the Dalai Lama raised his eyebrows. Then after some moments, he turned towards me with a thoughtful expression.

Yes indeed, I gazed at him evenly, with my coolest of blue expressions. I did try my best to tell you. But you just didn't seem able to perceive the horrors, despite the fact that they were shriekingly obvious. Litter tray, indeed!

We cats are the most versatile of creatures, who know exactly how to make ourselves at home in a great variety of places. It appeals to our enigmatic nature to be able to segue effortlessly from one role to another, manifesting intriguingly different identities, depending on where we are and what we are doing. That way we can never be pinned down. Categorized. Accused of being predictable in any way except, perhaps, of being utterly unpredictable.

Why else is it that so many cats are known by more than one name? In my case, as a sentinel on the Dalai Lama's windowsill, I am his 'Snow Lion'. On top of the filing cabinet in his Executive Assistants' office, I go by the more formal title of 'His Holiness' Cat' or HHC for short—His Holiness the Dalai Lama being referred to in official correspondence as HHDL. At The Himalaya Book Café, I am revered as 'Rinpoche', a Tibetan title meaning 'precious' and usually bestowed on much-loved lamas.

There is another place I like to appear, almost always at twilight, where an outdoor balcony offers the most magical view of the Himalaya mountains, their icy caps reflecting the gorgeous deepening colors of the setting sun. That place is The Downward Dog School of Yoga, and as its enlivening presence, I am known as 'Swami'. And yes, sometimes I am even garlanded with flowers.

I discovered the yoga studio one evening when I followed Serena after she left her day shift at The Himalaya Book Café. Intrigued by the way she transformed her appearance most evenings—emerging from the manager's office in black, bamboo yoga clothes, her hair pulled back in a ponytail—curiosity got the better of me. It was one of those long evenings when the Dalai Lama was away traveling, so I had nothing awaiting me at home.

I will never forget the scene that awaited me at the top of a steep hill on that first visit. There was a modest-looking bungalow with a sign spelled out in faded lettering: "The Downward Dog School of Yoga'. Inside was a small hallway, dominated by a shoe rack. Then, through a beaded curtain, a very large room, facing onto a panoramic vista of the Himalayas. Bi-fold doors, running the entire length of the facing side, had been pushed back. And there, posed in Virabhadrasana II or Warrior II, was a man with white, short-cropped hair, a tanned, timeless face and the most vibrant blue eyes.

"We seem to have a visitor," he had remarked, in his faint, German accent, having caught sight of me in the floor-to-ceiling mirror.

Even though cats weren't encouraged into the studio, I was given special dispensation, as Ludo instantly sensed a connection between us. Ludo had established the yoga studio in the early 60s. He had come to Dharamshala at the request of his friend Heinrich Harrer, of *Seven Years in Tibet* fame. Through Harrer, Ludo had been introduced to the Dalai Lama, who had encouraged him to set up the studio. The connection between Ludo and His Holiness went deeper than that, as I had discovered over the years, in a way which turned out to have particular significance for me.

A small, framed black and white photograph of a Lhasa Apso dog on the wall suggested why The Downward Dog School of Yoga had been so named. The little canine had belonged to the Dalai Lama back in 1959, when he was still living at the Potala Palace in Lhasa, Tibet. Through stray fragments of conversation, along with the most vividly real dreams, I had pieced together what had happened after that.

Forced to flee from Lhasa on foot, His Holiness asked a trusted female friend, Khandro-la, to take care of his much-loved dog. Initially it wasn't safe to take a dog on the perilous journey through the mountains, while being pursued by Red Army soldiers. But within a year, Khandro-la had entrusted the dog to the care of Norbu, a novice monk, who was joining a group leaving Tibet for India. Once he reached the safety of Dharamshala, Norbu would return the dog to the Dalai Lama.

However, that wasn't how things turned out.

Norbu and the group of monks were attacked by Chinese soldiers. Norbu was shot dead in his efforts to protect his precious cargo. It was left to one of his companions to cut the Lhasa Apso from the harness around Norbu's body.

Eventually, the group reached the safety of India. But when they arrived at Dharamshala, His Holiness was in Europe, trying to engage world leaders in the plight of his people. After an exchange of messages, it was agreed that Ludo would take care of the dog until the Dalai Lama returned home.

As it happened, the little dog had suffered from exposure on his way through the mountains and didn't have long to live. Within a few weeks he died.

When leaving Lhasa, the Dalai Lama had promised his pet that they would be reunited. And he didn't breach his promise, because the mind of that Lhasa Apso was reborn many years later in the form of a small kitten. One who His Holiness rescued from the streets of Delhi. One who came to acquire many special names and titles, not least of which are me, myself and I.

Yes, dear reader—a dog! No matter how many times I contemplate it, there is still disbelief that a feline so sumptuous and resplendent could ever have taken form as a scraggly mutt. But there is nothing like recognizing such a possibility to develop equanimity. How can you judge, hate or be hostile towards a group of beings, when you know you were one of them yourself? Perhaps not so very long ago?

The revelations I had pieced together about my past, while intriguing, had prompted even bigger questions. If I had been His Holiness' Dog until my death in 1960, and then had been reborn as His Holiness' Cat seven years ago, where had I been in the meantime? And, as importantly, who? The Dalai Lama hadn't had any animal companions in the intervening years. In what direction had my karma propelled me? Had I remained close to those with whom I had such strong bonds in this lifetime?

Questions of such a profound nature were often discussed on the balcony of The Downward Dog School of Yoga, a broad veranda beyond the glass doors that stretched the full length of the room. And it was here that I made my way that evening when I would otherwise have been alone—His Holiness being away on his travels.

It was a delightful, early summer's evening. The yoga class had just ended and several of Ludo's students had made their way out onto the balcony, as was their custom, to pour out beakers of green tea, relax among the assortment of rugs, cushions and bolsters, and take in the magnificence of the Himalaya mountains as they enacted their own nightly ritual. Their icy caps would reflect the colors of the sun in all its glory, beginning with a warm yellow which gradually deepened; and rivers flowed down the mountains, giving the impression of melting gold peaks ranged against a lapis blue sky.

As always, Ludo's students would sit around him, as conversation ranged effortlessly from the personal to the philosophical and back again. I would find myself a comfortable place to settle close to Serena or Ludo, beings with whom I had always felt a close affinity.

That evening, there was much excited talk about the legendary Yogi Tarchin, who had just completed his most recent solitary meditation retreat and had arrived in Dharamshala two evenings before. He was staying with good friends of Serena's, his long-term sponsors, the Cartright family.

"Is it true that he's totally clairvoyant?" Ewing, one of the longstanding class members, asked Serena.

"You've actually **met** Yogi Tarchin?" Flavia, who had only recently arrived from Brazil, gazed at Serena incredulously.

"I once heard a story," said Franc, owner of The Himalaya Book Café, "about how he can walk at superhuman speeds."

"It's called *lung-gom-pa*," observed Ludo. "A practice of highly realized masters."

Serena glanced around at the expectant faces. "I've heard a lot of stories about Yogi Tarchin. Never from him, of course, he never talks of such things …"

"A master never reveals his *siddhis*," confirmed Ludo. "His magic powers."

"But having known him since I was about ten," continued Serena. "I have no doubt that he perceives things that most people cannot. He has developed in his meditative concentration so much that he is able to clear his mind. He is clear-sighted—isn't that the meaning of clairvoyance?" she looked around

On the balcony, the others were nodding.

"What you're saying ..." Flavia looked from Serena to Ludo, "is that these special powers, these *siddhis*, are not like a special gift? They're not something you're born with? Any person can develop them?"

"Some persons are born with these abilities," confirmed Ludo, in his somewhat formal manner. "But they also arise naturally among those who develop their concentration."

"So we could all study to become clairvoyant?"

Ludo moved his head from side to side, equivocally. "We don't set out to become clairvoyant. That is not the goal. That is," he shrugged, "merely a side effect. We set out to develop our concentration. Greater concentration means less agitation. For most of us, our minds are like snow globes," he imitated shaking a globe in his hand. "Constant thoughts, feelings, impulses. But great meditation masters like Yogi Tarchin, who are able to settle their minds, have a very different experience of reality."

While Ludo's students absorbed his words in silence, I looked up at the mountains, watching the molten gold peaks gradually turn to cerise as the sun slipped over the opposite horizon.

Ludo continued, "In the words of the unequaled Tilopa:
Gazing intently into the empty sky, vision ceases;
Likewise, when mind gazes into mind itself,
The train of discursive and conceptual thought ends
And supreme enlightenment is gained."

For a while, it was as though everyone on the balcony was held in that particular moment, free from thought and bathed in the radiant glow of twilight. Even in that evanescent moment, there was a sense of timelessness, of infinite possibility, as though Tilopa's words had themselves evoked a glimpse of the transcendence of which they spoke.

After a long while Serena observed, "Such beautiful words."

Others murmured in agreement, before Flavia said, "It seems that clairvoyance and other siddhis are not something we try to gain. They are what happens when we let go."

"Exactly!" agreed Ludo. "We all need to let go—especially of our preoccupations with ourselves."

"The cause of all our heartache," agreed Serena with feeling.

I remembered her recent visit to His Holiness. How apologetic she had been at losing her temper. How the truth of all her unhappiness had come pouring out.

I also recollected the Dalai Lama explaining how our inner journey of development only started when we accepted responsibility for the causes of our own feelings, which weren't out there in the world, however much we might believe this—and perhaps even want to believe it—but within our own hearts and minds. And how renunciation meant turning away from these true causes of unhappiness. The first paw of spiritual success.

"There is much wisdom in letting go," observed Ludo.

"And peace too," Serena agreed.

An evening breeze rippled up the Kangra valley, bringing with it the scents not only of Himalaya pine, but also a medley of evening meals being prepared in the homes around us. Most of the students were getting up and leaving, bringing palms to their hearts and murmuring a grateful *namaste* to Ludo as they departed.

Serena and Franc remained where they were, and so did I, in no great hurry to go anywhere, especially while the mountains, possessing a living, breathing presence of their own, settled into the deepening twilight, their peaks darkening in color through deep red into crimson.

"One of my favorite places in the world," Serena gestured from where she was leaning against the balcony rails towards where successive ranges of mountains dissolved away to infinity.

The other two followed her gaze and, after a while, Ludo confided, "Before I go, I would very much like to know this place can continue without me."

"Go where?" asked Franc.

Ludo turned to him with a surprised expression. "Die," he said, with Teutonic candor.

"But you're still so vital," said Serena, flicking her fingers upwards energetically.

"I am 75," said Ludo. "In good health now. But what of the future? Who will take over running the studio when I am no longer able?"

"You have very accomplished students."

Ludo nodded. "It is my privilege," he agreed. "But each one of them has their own life and work and family. Managing a studio like this is a full-time occupation."

Serena and Franc considered this in silence.

"There is also the matter of trust. Many very capable yoga teachers pass through these doors every year."

It was true. His Holiness acted like a magnet not only to devoted Buddhists, but to spiritual seekers of all kinds, including those for whom yoga was a precious form of meditation. Many of them found their way, sometime during their stay, to The Downward Dog School of Yoga.

"Many are well-intentioned and would like to stay on. But do they have a head for business, because that is also necessary? Could one be sure they would follow the practices that our students value?"

In the semi-darkness, Ludo began to chuckle. "There is another way to look at things. When I spoke earlier about letting go, I was partly talking to myself. We teach what we most need to learn, yes? I tell myself I want to ensure that my students are cared for. But maybe the real reason has to do with my own ego."

"Ah, yes!" agreed Serena. "A slippery creature. Expert at clothing its true intentions beneath those which seem more noble."

"I find myself wondering about that often," said Franc, unusually subdued. "I tell myself I'm doing something for a compassionate reason, but then I doubt myself. You know, the Franc who arrived in Dharamshala—the old Franc—was only interested in being different. I was into the whole Buddhist shtick. The blessing strings and initiations. The mala beads and shaven head. The craving to come across as someone special. But then I met Geshe Wangpo, and realized how pointless that whole act was. Nobody really cares if you're a Buddhist— especially not Buddhists. Who was I trying to impress? I came to realize that it's all about inner transformation and I started trying to make some changes in my life."

In the yoga studio there was a movement, as the beaded curtain was parted and someone stepped inside, pausing momentarily before heading out towards the balcony where we sat together. The darkness seemed to be making it easier for Franc to confess.

"Lately I've been wondering if I've really changed that much. I find myself thinking the same, self-centered, ultimately destructive things that old Franc used to think. Or like you say, Ludo, telling myself I'm doing something for one reason, when the real reason is probably another. Just like it's always been."

"I'm sure you're speaking for us all, Franc." Serena was sympathetic.

"True inner change ..." confirmed Ludo, "is a lifetime's practice."

"Hmm," Franc sounded unconvinced. "It's been a real downer. I haven't been able to read any of my Dharma texts for months. My meditations are all over the place. Sometimes I wonder why I even bother."

"Have you spoken to Geshe Wangpo?" asked Ludo.

Franc snorted. The Namgyal lama was famous for his powerful presence and intolerance of laxity. "I know what he would tell me," he said, imitating him, "**More** enthusiasm, **more** patience is necessary!"

Twilight had deepened and the balcony was now in near darkness, apart from where light from the studio spilled outside. With the sun having performed its final salutation, the ice caps of the Himalayas had turned to silver, their liquid peaks catching the ethereal luminescence of the rising moon.

After the longest while Franc said, "I only wish I could find a way to bring my Dharma practice back to life."

There was a pause before a warm and somewhat mischievous voice came from across the balcony. "You should be careful what you wish for."

It was Serena who first recognized the unexpected visitor. "Yogi Tarchin!" she exclaimed, rising to her feet and hurrying to meet him.

A slight figure dressed in a light shirt with a Nehru collar, cotton pants and bare feet, having left his shoes at the entrance, Yogi Tarchin looked no different from any of the other men you might pass on a Dharamshala evening. However, the power of his presence was instant and unmistakable. The moment his eyes met Serena's, his face lit up with such warmth that joy seemed to burst across the balcony and out into the evening, to encompass even the Himalayas.

As the two of them were hugging, Ludo and Franc rose to their feet. "No, please stay!" urged their visitor, but to no avail. The two men were soon each embracing him warmly, the contagion of happiness touching all of our hearts.

Yogi Tarchin looked down to where I, too, had joined them. "I see that His Holiness' Cat remains a constant presence," his goatee beard moved as he chuckled.

"We were just talking about you," said Ludo. "We'd heard you'd finished your retreat and were back in town. Can I offer you some tea?"

Yogi Tarchin bowed his head, "Thank you, Ludo. But I am here only to deliver a message to Serena."

Ludo and Franc glanced over at Serena—as I did. A message from Yogi Tarchin, at the end of a three-year retreat! Was he about to reveal some profound insight? A startling revelation made possible only by his clairvoyance? An arcane or esoteric truth?

Picking up on our thoughts, Yogi Tarchin met Serena's sparkling eyes. "From your mother."

Serena's eyebrows shot upwards.

"She'd like to borrow a blender from The Himalaya Book Café and she wonders if you can help her prepare dinner at the Cartrights' this evening?"

Serena was shaking her head, eyes burning with disbelief at the mundanity of his errand. "Only my mother! I'm so sorry, Rinpoche. She shouldn't be treating you like a messenger."

He chuckled, shrugging with an easy lightness. "Your mother has been a good friend for many years. It's a beautiful evening for a walk." With a sweep of the hand he seemed to encompass the soaring mountains, the squares of light appearing in homes down the valley, the warmth of the night air with its subtle aroma of Himalaya pine. As was so often the case in the presence of Yogi Tarchin, there was a feeling of time somehow existing on a different and paused dimension of infinite wellbeing.

He took a step back, bringing his palms to his heart. "Thank you, thank you," he glanced towards each of us.

"I suppose I'd better be on my way," said Serena, gesturing to acknowledge Yogi Tarchin's message.

Yogi Tarchin turned to leave, walking across the studio accompanied by Serena and Ludo. Pushing through the bead curtain he paused, while Serena slipped on her sandals. Turning to Ludo he said, "I hope you will join us for dinner?"

Ludo's face lit up with delight at the unexpected invitation. "That would be wonderful!" he said. "Enlightened guests accompanied by the Trincis' heavenly cooking—mother and daughter. You know, they are the best European chefs in the whole of Himachal Pradesh!"

"I have no doubt," Rinpoche chuckled, reaching out to squeeze Ludo's arm. "Reminder of the old country?"

"Very much so."

"Perhaps," Rinpoche looked at him significantly for a moment, "it's time for you to take a most well-deserved vacation in Germany."

Ludo looked surprised; Rinpoche offered direct suggestions, like this one, only rarely. And when he did, it was safe to assume he was doing so for reasons which, as a yogi, were much more obvious to him than to most beings.

After a pause Ludo murmured, "My sister has been trying to persuade me to do that for the past few years. Perhaps it's time."

"Family," Rinpoche nodded significantly. "Very important. Isn't it, HHC?" Bending to rub my chest, he asked softly, "And all is well at home, Serena?"

She nodded. "Sid and I got married when you were on retreat."

"And Zahra. Growing up, yes?" It seemed more like an observation than a question.

Serena chuckled. "Yes. She's a real teenager now!"

He used his fingernails to massage my forehead, just the way I liked it, before standing upright. "I see that mother and daughter are close."

"Is that twilight language you're using, Rinpoche?" Serena slipped a fleece around her shoulders. She was referring to the cryptic way that Tibetan Buddhists sometimes speak, using symbols and metaphors to conceal what they really mean beneath a veil of alternative references.

"Oh, no. Quite literal."

Really, I wondered? Who was the mother and who the daughter in this scenario?

Ludo waved them goodbye, as they made their way out of the building and into the street.

"I'm so pleased you're back in Dharamshala, Rinpoche," Serena hugged him before turning to leave. "I've missed you, even though you're always …" she touched her heart.

He brought his palms to his forehead and when he looked at her it was as if waves of oceanic, unconditional love rushed from his heart towards her.

As they went their separate ways he called out, almost as an afterthought, "See you soon! And happy birthday, to all beings born on this day."

Several days later, I was taking my regular mid-morning nap on top of the filing cabinet in the Executive Assistants' office, when I was woken by the faint but unmistakable aroma of Kouros aftershave. Raising my head I parsed the air, before hopping onto Tenzin's desk, making sure, as I made my way to the edge of the desk, that I glided my sumptuously bushy tail over the back of his hands as he worked on a keyboard. I was soon on my way downstairs.

Sure enough, when I arrived in the kitchen, it was to find the external doors open and Franc carrying crates of fresh vegetables in from a van in the courtyard. A few moments later, Serena followed him inside carrying another crate. They were evidently stocking up ahead of a VIP meal.

"Whew!" Serena exclaimed, after they'd finished offloading several more cartons, boxes and trays of condiments.

Perched on a small set of steps, my regular kitchen viewing platform, I watched her wipe her brow with the back of her hand, glancing at Franc. "Drink?"

"A glass of water," he nodded.

She placed two glasses on the counter, before opening the fridge door.

"You okay?" asked Franc.

"Sure. Why?" Pouring out the water, she handed him a glass.

Franc took a long draft before saying, 'You just seem different today. Jauntier."

Serena gave him a quizzical smile. "That obvious, huh?"

"Go on," he prompted, a secretive smile playing across his own features. "Spill the beans."

"I've just landed a major contract for the spice packs," her grin widened. "This company, they used to be a competitor, were having problems sourcing product. They've got great distribution. We've got plenty of product, but hassles with distribution."

"Match made in heaven?"

"It is!" she was shaking her head. "And it's all happened so suddenly. I'm still processing it, but it's like this huge relief."

"I can see," nodded Frank. "And I'm very happy for you. How did you conjure up the deal?"

She paused for a moment, brow furrowing for a moment before telling him, "That's the weirdest bit. You see, it was all down to Yogi Tarchin. Something he said the other night."

"At yoga?" Franc's expression turned curious.

Serena nodded. "I was on my way out and he called out something about happy birthday to anyone born on that day. It seemed kind of spontaneous. Quirky. You know, that's Rinpoche."

Franc was nodding.

"Later that night, I got a social media reminder that it was Dionné Delaney's birthday. The two of us used to work together back in London. She's still there. We used to be friendly but weren't that close. Usually I wouldn't have paid any attention to the Happy Birthday reminder thing but, of course, this time I did. I sent her a one-liner.

"Next thing I knew she'd sent me a message, and I checked out her profile and found she'd moved to this food company as head of their retail products. They were planning to pull their whole spice range off the market because of product shortages. But now …" Serena glowed with excitement.

Franc was shaking his head. "Who would have thought such massive change could come about because of a single yoga class."

"I know," agreed Serena, before catching something in his expression. "What?"

Franc was nodding, "You're not the only one who's had a Yogi Tarchin experience."

"You too? What did he say?"

"Be careful what you wish for."

"I remember," she was nodding. "On the balcony. What was all that about?"

"I didn't know at the time. He seemed to be kind of directing it at me. That night when I went to sleep I had the most hyperreal dreams and Yogi Tarchin was right there, by my side, guiding me through. Well, he had the appearance of Manjushri, but I knew it was Yogi Tarchin."

"Incredible! Where did he take you?"

"Two places. Sets of places, really. First we were in this unbelievable, war zone place, where people were being flung to the ground, having lines burned into their bodies with metal ropes, then being dismembered by monster-like creatures."

Serena pulled a face.

"Throughout the whole thing, Yogi Tarchin kept repeating the same phrase: *Body not necessary. Body not necessary.* It segued to this furnace. We were walking through it and Yogi Tarchin was pointing at this and that. I've got no idea what he was trying to show me. Then I heard these faint, wailing noises. I realized there were actual beings somehow there in the fire. You could hardly tell them apart from the flames. It was like they were being permanently tortured."

"A nightmare about hell realms?"

Franc nodded, "That's how it started. But it suddenly changed and we were in deva realms with palatial homes and the most unbelievably beautiful people, and all they needed to do was blink and whatever they wanted just manifested. Yogi Tarchin was still with me all the way saying: *Body not necessary.* We were in this place, still very beautiful, where some of the wisest of the beautiful people were praying for human rebirth. There was no incentive to develop spiritually in this place, and no teachings. It was all wonderful, but completely pointless."

Franc stared at Serena. "It's still really vivid in my mind. Like I can close my eyes and be back there."

"And … there was a point? For you?"

"Completely! Along with what was happening, I was understanding things. When Yogi Tarchin was saying *body not necessary*, what he meant was that even though I was having these really vivid experiences, my body wasn't involved. Part of me knew that my body was lying in bed at home. But I could smell the burning flesh of the torturers. I could hear the music made by the flowers in the gardens of the beautiful realms.

45

Everything looked and felt completely real.

"That's when I understood that when we die, even if we don't have a body, our mind endures. Just like when we're dreaming we can experience anything and everything as realistically as if we were awake. More so. It's like this hyperreality. And our mind is producing it. Whatever arises in our mind is what we experience. There's no body to tether us to a different reality. Our reality is whatever our mind projects. Nothing else."

Serena was nodding.

"Which made me realize that when we lose this human body," he was shaking his head, "all we're taking with us is our mind and our mental habits. None of our belongings or achievements or reputation have any value from the moment we die. The only thing that matters is how we're used to thinking."

Taking this all in, Serena said after a while, "Yogi Tarchin said: *Be careful what you wish for.*" Franc nodded.

"What did you wish for?"

"Remember on the balcony I was telling you and Ludo how I'd hit a brick wall with my practice. Couldn't get motivated." Franc looked rueful. "It was only after I woke up I remembered saying how I wished I could find a way to bring my Dharma practice back to life."

"Sounds like you don't have a problem in that department anymore," Serena's eyes twinkled.

"When you experience something like that, firsthand, it really brings it home to you how extraordinary this life is, **we** are. What an amazing opportunity to shape our future."

Serena smiled.

On the kitchen steps, I meowed softly.

"Yes," said Serena. "Amazing. All of it. Especially the beings we meet along the way."

Later that evening, it happened again. This time the invaders were so audacious they didn't even wait till midnight. His Holiness was having his early evening catch-up with Tenzin and Oliver when the squealing began. At full volume.

Instantly I leapt up from where I'd been resting on the windowsill. Fur bristling, I crossed the room. There were three grown men sitting right there, each one of them wide awake. Surely they weren't going to just sit around doing nothing, while rats rampaged downstairs?

They carried on talking, ignoring the racket. Talking earnestly about His Holiness' forthcoming visit to New York, as if everything was perfectly normal.

I unleashed a long, low, threatening meow and the men glanced over.

"What's the matter, HHC?" asked Tenzin.

The rodent squeals were growing in number and volume. After a few moments, when none of the men showed the slightest inclination to act, I began clawing at the door, just as I had done a few nights before.

As on that occasion, the Dalai Lama got up, came over and reached towards me. Unlike before, however, I was prepared for what came next. As soon as I felt his hands reach around me I leapt from his clutches, scampered across the room and darted

47

under the desk, to the spot where I knew his arm couldn't reach, no matter how hard he tried to stretch. That's if he felt inclined to try and catch me. Which, on this occasion, he did not.

I waited a while for him to return to his meeting, wondering why on earth all three men were willing to turn a blind ear to the pillage and destruction a short distance below. As I emerged from under the desk and returned to where they were engrossed in travel planning, the rodent shrieking abruptly changed from excitement to fear. Before stopping altogether.

A few moments later, there was a frenzied knocking on the door. Oliver rose to let in a distraught Mrs. Trinci. "They've come again!" she wailed, raising arms to her head, bracelets clanking heavily as she did. "Rats! I caught them at it. A dozen of them! *Mamma mia*! They have ruined the sponges for tomorrow's trifle!"

Even though Mrs. Trinci's volcanic temperament had settled in recent years, she was still a force of nature, those heavily mascaraed lashes framing eyes which blazed with a passion unlike anything else witnessed at Namgyal Monastery.

"I'm so sorry, Mrs. Trinci." The Dalai Lama apologized as if he had personally encouraged the rats.

"Oh no, no Your Holiness. It's not your fault." She shot a glance to where I was sitting in the middle of the carpet. "If my little *tesorina*—my little treasure—had been there, one look and they would have been gone!"

After a pause, Tenzin pointed out, "She **was** scratching at the door."

The Dalai Lama was nodding. "And she also did this earlier in the week. She woke me in the middle of the night and was very agitated. Was it Tuesday when the rats got into the pantry?"

"*Si, si*," nodded Mrs Trinci.

As all of them turned to look at me, it was Tenzin who spoke in a reverential tone. "Perhaps HHC is clairvoyant?"

Then after a moment of further reflection, "What if she is not, in fact, a cat at all?"

Oh yes! I thought. What a splendid idea! Buddhas and bodhisattvas are known to be able to manifest in any form that may benefit beings. What if I truly was a bodhi**catt**va, a delightful fluffy manifestation of the mind of enlightenment? **This** was a thought I could get used to!

"I think there could be a more mundane explanation," said Oliver.

All eyes turned to him, including my own, icy-blue ones.

"A cat's senses are quite different from ours," he said. "They can hear two octaves higher than we can. So it's quite possible that she was hearing the rats on both occasions. She probably wondered why we didn't do anything to stop them."

I wasn't sure how to take this information. As intrigued as I was by the idea that I could hear things that humans could not, I preferred the more exalted explanation.

"You might say that she is clairaudient," observed the Dalai Lama, rescuing me from my dilemma. "If a person had the hearing range of HHC, we would say they were superhuman."

"With ultrasonic hearing," agreed Oliver.

"Like Superman," offered Tenzin.

"With secret powers," chuckled His Holiness.

That evening, when we had our personal time together, I was perched at the end of the bed, paws tucked underneath. His Holiness put down the book he was reading for a moment and looked over at me. "What a wonderful variety of consciousnesses there are in this world, Snow Lion."

I knew he was referring to the conversation earlier that evening, about the rats and me.

"Some see their own perceptions as ordinary. To others, that makes them extraordinary. Most important of all is that each one of us has the capacity to develop our minds, to cultivate our abilities, so that we can help others as well as ourselves."

I looked up at him as he spoke. For me, his voice was the most deeply comforting sound in the world.

"What a terrible waste to think of oneself as only ordinary, when the opposite is true. Not to realize the precious opportunity this lifetime gives us. Renunciation is not only about turning **away** from the causes of our suffering; it is also about turning **towards** becoming who we really are. Transcending the ordinary. Realizing our own Buddha nature."

I thought of Franc's dream-time journey through different realms, his direct experience that mind and mental habits are all that endure. Of Serena's recognition that the cause of her former unhappiness didn't come from outside her, but from within—and that as soon as she had begun to let go of her attachment, her experience of reality began to change.

Where did 'inner' end and 'outer' begin? Did this explain Franc saying that "reality is whatever our mind projects?" And is this why the experience of an enlightened being, no matter what the circumstances, is said to be ever-increasing bliss?

The Dalai Lama carefully closed the book he was reading, placed it on his bedside table and folded his hands together at his heart. "This is why we take refuge in the Buddha, Dharma and Sangha," he murmured, closing his eyes. "We are saying, "Yes, I have Buddha nature. I possess a mind capable of full enlightenment. And I will attain it, both for my own sake as well as for all others, equally and without exception." This is the first step of our spiritual journey. The first of four aspects. And we see it every time we look at an image of a Buddha."

Do we, I wondered? Since the first time His Holiness had mentioned it, I had spent time studying Buddha statues and wall-hangings and, for the life of me, I couldn't see four of anything. It wasn't like the Buddhas held four particular things in their hands, or had four separate ornaments. Whatever these four things were, they remained an enigma—one I hoped would be revealed in time.

For a few moments he sat in silent meditation. Well, not complete silence, because at the foot of the bed I was purring appreciatively. Could there be a more appropriate soundtrack by which to contemplate the mind of enlightenment?

The Dalai Lama leaned to turn off the light.

"Goodnight, my little bodhicattva," he murmured, as he did at this moment every night.

As always, I purred till we were both asleep.

The next morning, the Dalai Lama was at his desk when Tenzin showed in an unexpected visitor.

"I don't want to take up your time. I'm on my way home for a few weeks and just came to say goodbye." It was Ludo, who would make such courtesy calls to his dear friend every few years, whenever he left Dharamshala for a while.

His Holiness got up from where he was sitting and the two men bowed towards each other, foreheads touching in affectionate respect.

"I think it will be a good trip," the Dalai Lama told Ludo. "Most useful!"

Usefulness was among the greatest virtues, as far as the Dalai Lama was concerned.

I remembered Yogi Tarchin's advice to Ludo on the balcony of The Downward Dog School of Yoga. It seemed that he wasn't wasting any time acting on it.

Ludo only stayed for a few minutes, to exchange news of mutual friends in Germany before excusing himself, stepping backwards to the door, in the traditional Tibetan show of respect.

From my windowsill a short while later, I watched him emerge from the building, cross the courtyard, and climb into the back of a waiting taxi.

How much had changed since that evening on the yoga studio balcony only days before, I mused. Serena was now a woman unburdened, having found a way to resolve her business problems. Franc had been well and truly jolted from his lethargy regarding his Dharma practice. Ludo was on his way back to his roots for a well-earned holiday. Which only left Yogi Tarchin's cryptic observation directed at me, that mother and daughter had become close.

On that crystal clear Himalaya morning, as I observed the circadian rhythm playing out once again on the Namgyal courtyard, I wondered what on earth he could have been referring to? And, precisely, to whom?

CHAPTER THREE

As a cat of many names, you might imagine that yet another title would be of little consequence to a feline so admired as I am. You might imagine that, dear reader—but you would be wrong.

Because, unlike all the other names bestowed on me, this particular one was different. It wasn't conferred on me because of who I live with (HHC), or by a quirk of circumstance (Swami), or even on account of my extraordinary good genes (The Most Beautiful Creature That Ever Lived). No, this was a designation I earned. A calling to which I was inspired. And it is one of the titles that makes me profoundly happy—a quality of happiness quite different from the rush of gluttonous good feeling which overwhelms me when presented by Mrs. Trinci with a bowl of diced chicken liver.

My new vocation is one which would simply never have happened had I not wandered across the courtyard to Namgyal temple one balmy Tuesday night.

I would like to tell you that it was the lure of a teaching by Geshe Wangpo, one of the most respected lamas at Namgyal Monastery, which drew me from my windowsill that evening. Alas, it was simple curiosity.

Although Franc and Serena had both been regulars at Geshe-la's Tuesday night classes in the past, during recent months their attendance had become much less regular. I was intrigued to know whether the experiences sparked by Yogi Tarchin in the past week would see them return to their temple cushions.

Leaving His Holiness in deep discussion with Oliver about the translation of a new book, I made my way downstairs, over the paved courtyard and up the steps into the temple. I hopped on a shelf at the back which I had made my own over the years, from where I could survey all the goings-on in this extraordinary room.

Evenings were my favorite temple time. When all was dark outside, the sea of butter lamp offerings at the front of the room would bring the golden faces of the Buddha statues to life in their flickering light. The wall-hangings and decorations would gently sway in the evening breeze, energizing the room with prana. It was as though you could **feel** the presence of countless Buddhas and bodhisattvas in this special place. There was an energy, a sense of the presence of enlightened minds drawn to these sacred objects and practices, like geese to a lotus lake. And as more and more people arrived, taking their places on maroon-colored meditation cushions, that feeling of openness, of contact, grew all the more.

Geshe Wangpo's Tuesday night classes were based on the Lamrim, or Path to Enlightenment, the core text in the sutra tradition of His Holiness' lineage. While most of those attending were Namgyal monks, the talks were also available to ordinary residents from Dharamshala. I knew a number of these. Sam, manager of the bookstore section at The Himalaya Book Café, and his Canadian wife, Bronnie, were there. Ewing Klipspringer and Merrilee from yoga class—no Ludo this evening, of course, although he was a regular. Serena arrived soon after I had settled. She was a different version of the person who had been so stressed out when she'd stormed away from the Dalai Lama. It was as if that event had made inevitable a change she had long needed to make—letting go. Franc wasn't that long behind her, making his way to a cushion near hers. I noticed the two of them exchange a smile.

When Geshe Wangpo appeared through the front door of the temple, the low-level murmur of voices around the temple immediately stopped, replaced by a hushed reverence. A round, muscular man with the physical frame of many Tibetans, along with an extraordinary power, he communicated another engaging quality—profound kindness.

Geshe Wangpo took his place on the teaching throne. After the regular lamrim chants and everyone had settled their minds in meditation, he looked around at all the expectant faces. "Tonight I want to talk about the practice at the heart of Tibetan Buddhism," he said. "About what sets it apart from other traditions, including other Buddhist lineages. We have many wonderful practices, or mental tools, to use. Different practices for people with different temperaments. This is not a one-size-fits-all tradition!"

There were a few chuckles from around the room. When I thought about the personalities of Franc, Ludo, Mrs. Trinci and Oliver, I realized how very different they all were—and yet how each one of their lives had been transformed by the different Dharma methods they had adopted.

"No matter what you like to do, which particular meditations or activities, they are all of limited value unless motivated by this one, central practice."

Geshe Wangpo had a way of presenting the teachings so that you wanted to keep on listening. As though narrating an unfolding story, he would keep his audience in suspense. Even if they thought they knew what was coming, he still had them on the edge of their cushions, as they awaited confirmation.

"In Buddhism, we define love as the wish to give happiness to others. It is a universal truth that if we wish for happiness ourselves, we should seek ways to give it to others. In giving we receive."

He surveyed the rows of monks and townspeople sitting before him in rapt attention. "But love is not the practice I want to talk about tonight." There was a twinkle about his features, as he drew everyone in the room to him.

"In Buddhism, we define compassion as the wish to free others from suffering. Based on love, if we wish for the happiness of others but see them troubled or defeated, upset or abandoned, or in any kind of difficulty, the cultivation of compassion is what motivates us to help. Without compassion, we remain indifferent. With compassion, we develop empathy. We can imagine what it's like to be them and wish to free them from their suffering, as though we are suffering ourselves. But again, beautiful as it is," he paused. "Cultivating compassion is not the practice I want to talk about tonight."

The roar of a Harley-Davidson, thundering along a nearby street, disturbed the peace of the temple. But after the din had passed, the silence that followed was all the more deeply felt, like the effect of a thunderstorm clearing the air. Or the relief and tranquility, after a shrill car alarm is switched off. For a few moments, oceanic peace.

"The reason I began with love and compassion is that they are the foundations of the practice I **do** want to discuss. The whole basis of our central motivation.

"As ordinary beings, there are limits to the help we can offer others. We may support a friend through a loss or disappointment. But we can't prevent them from experiencing future losses and disappointments. We may offer financial support to those in need. But no amount of money can protect them from emotional setbacks, for example, or illness.

"The problems of our lives are many and varied. Each one of us has to deal with constant change. For as long as we are caught up in the conventional reality of birth, aging, sickness and death, we have to live with unpredictability and challenge. We have to live with the only certainty that, some day in the future, we will definitely lose everything we possess, every being whom we cherish, every accomplishment we may treasure, and move on from this lifetime, never to experience reality this way again.

"For Tibetan Buddhists, this is not acceptable. Not for ourselves. Not for others. We want to provide more than temporary support for others. More than limited help. What we seek is a **permanent** solution."

As I glanced about the temple, I observed how all eyes were fixed on Geshe Wangpo with an air of keen expectation.

"The reason why Buddha is said to be enlightened is because he found a way to achieve lasting fulfillment and freedom. Two millennia before quantum science, Buddha established that what we take to be concrete reality is, in reality, a projection of mind itself. Change our mind, and we change our experience. You may say that Buddha created the ultimate self-development program, because through it we are able to transcend conventional reality, ordinary life and death, and attain states of ever-increasing bliss.

"This is what we seek, for both ourselves and for others. Not short-term fixes, working with a flawed model of reality, but a permanent solution based on the way that things truly are."

Geshe-la leaned forward in his seat, his voice deepening for extra emphasis. "When we seek enlightenment for the sake of all beings, this is called *bodhicitta*. It is our central practice. Based on the wish to give happiness to others and to free them from suffering, not only in the short term, but permanently, bodhicitta is our life's purpose. We wish to achieve Buddhahood to help all other living beings attain this same state. This is the most altruistic, the most panoramic intention ever conceived."

A wave of upliftment passed through the temple, as well as smiles from those who had anticipated Geshe Wangpo's conclusion.

"Not only is bodhicitta the most altruistic purpose. It is a direct cause of enlightenment in itself." Looking about his audience with a gentle smile, the lama asked, "Why might that be?"

From the front row there were murmured answers before a monk replied, quite clearly, "Karma."

Geshe Wangpo was nodding his head. "Good point," he agreed. "When we are motivated by bodhicitta, the same action brings dramatically increased results. Remember, two of the things that give karma its weight are the object and, importantly, the intention.

"Bodhicitta is the greatest purifier of negativities, the most powerful creator of merit, because the **object** of our motivation is every single living being throughout universal space. We don't just wish to help one person, or a group of people, or other beings. No! **All** living beings, who are without number." He allowed this point time to penetrate the minds of all present.

"As for intention, it is their enlightenment we seek—a motivation which cannot be surpassed. We don't merely wish for the sick to be healed, or the poor to have their needs met, or the miserable to find comfort. Our concern is not only for their needs in this lifetime here and now, but for them to be **permanently** free from samsara, for them to achieve complete and perfect enlightenment. So powerful is bodhicitta, it is said that the karmic effects of giving even a single seed to a bird to eat, with genuine bodhicitta motivation, are incalculable."

"So, yes," Geshe Wangpo turned back to the monk. "Karma is one reason why bodhicitta propels us to enlightenment. But are there others?"

In the past I had noticed how Geshe Wangpo liked to involve his students on such evenings, rather than deliver long teachings. The result was more of a conversation than a lecture. Interaction and the chance to engage.

Among the answers to his most recent question was an inaudible reply, to which he responded, "Exactly! As we think, so we become. By becoming very familiar with bodhicitta, by applying it constantly to our actions throughout the day, we train our minds, step by step. We become strongly acquainted with the mind of enlightenment, as it's also known.

"Initially, we may do only the same things we did before, but strive to recollect bodhicitta motivation. For example, when making a friend a cup of tea or dropping a coin in the charity box, we recollect: *May this action be the cause for my enlightenment for the sake of all living beings.* The more we repeat this so it becomes part of habitual thinking, the more the mask becomes the person. This is Buddhist psychology," he smiled. "In the West they call it modeling—where we model our behavior on the example of someone who has already achieved what we wish to achieve. Same, same."

"But I feel like such a fraud when I do that," interjected the distinctive Tennessee accent of Merrilee, a long-term student of Ludo's at The Downward Dog School of Yoga. "I was going to drop a coin in the box anyway."

Geshe Wangpo looked in her direction and nodded. "In the initial stages, we have to fabricate our bodhicitta." He paused for a moment before delivering a mischievous smile, "Fake it till you make it!"

There was scattered laughter around the room.

"Understanding the meaning of bodhicitta is actually a life time's practice. But we need to start where we are. Over time, by listening, thinking and meditating, our conviction in bodhicitta deepens to the point where it becomes heartfelt. Spontaneous. That's when our actions become a true source of joy, both to self and others."

For a few moments everyone in the gompa absorbed his words in silence, the only sound coming from the gentle thuds made by the bottom rails of thangkas, buffeted against the walls in the breeze coming through the windows.

The silence was broken by a lone voice, "Who am I to become enlightened?"

It was a young man who gave voice to these words, a backpacker from Europe by the look of him, who I hadn't seen in the temple before. Sitting tall on his meditation cushion, with tousled dark hair, olive skin and finely sculpted features, he had an aura of melancholy about him.

Geshe Wangpo fixed him with a gaze of deep compassion, before replying, "Who are you not to? The Buddha was once an ordinary man. He had his failings. Fortunately for us, not only did he attain enlightenment, but he showed us the most rapid way to attain the same state." Geshe Wangpo paused as he held the man's gaze, and it seemed to me he was somehow guided to share what he said next.

"The idea you may have of yourself as someone who may not be capable of enlightenment—that's just an idea. A thought. A concept. There is no concrete reality to it whatsoever. So," he shrugged, "because it does not serve you well, let go of it. Do not energize it with the power of your attention. Do not dignify it with a substantiality that it does not, in fact, possess."

As so often happens when listening to highly realized lamas, in the temple with Geshe Wangpo on Tuesday nights, enlightenment did seem to be something that was accessible, something that was just there, within grasp, as simple as stepping from one room into another. No doubt this had as much to do with Geshe-la's presence as with his teachings. By conveying a glimpse of the feeling of what enlightenment might be like, you found that all your normal preoccupations, your usual thoughts, dissolved away, and instead you experienced a feeling of deep and timeless peace.

That feeling, and the wisdom of bodhicitta that inspired it, stayed with me in the days that followed.

A few mornings later, I hopped onto the sill and was taking in the morning sights and scents, when I suddenly became aware of a bewitching fragrance. An aroma that had once been a familiar part of my life—but not for some months. Something I'd forgotten about but, now reminded, I simply had to investigate.

I made my way downstairs, across the courtyard and out the gates. This morning, instead of turning right to go down to The Himalaya Book Café, I headed in the opposite direction. A short distance along the road, on the same side as Namgyal Monastery, there was a small garden, and just beyond that, a nursing home. I'd been acquainted with the garden since my early days of living with the Dalai Lama. It was just a short distance from the veranda of the nursing home and was beautifully tended, with lush garden beds, a neatly trimmed lawn and a stately cedar tree at its center, beneath which was a wooden bench, rarely used.

I had discovered that the person who kept this place so immaculately tended was none other than the man I had regarded as my nemesis, during my earliest days at Namgyal Monastery: His Holiness' Driver. A large man, powerfully built, the Driver had initially struck me as a rough and ready type, lacking in all the diplomatic niceties of the rest of the household. On one of my very first days at Namgyal, when I'd heard a mouse beneath the floorboards of our building, I had managed to catch it, returning in triumph to the Executive Assistants' office with the beast in my mouth. While everyone else had scurried into action to rescue the mouse—still very much alive—wringing their hands over my misdemeanor, it had been His Holiness' Driver who had taken one look at me and suggested a nickname: Mousie Tung.

It was a nickname I hated, from the first moment I heard it. And in that same instant, because it was so monstrously appropriate, I felt it might stick. Being associated with such evil horrified me! Stalking away in high dudgeon, it had been the Driver, rather than my own enslavement to instinct, that I'd resented. Even though I had lost sight of the principle of non-harmfulness during my time beneath the floorboards, it was so much easier just to blame the Driver. Fortunately for me, the nickname didn't become more widely used. He was the only one who ever used it.

As the years went by and I got to know him better, I had come to see the Driver in a very different light. While he was large and overwhelming, especially to a small cat with wonky pins, he was also extremely kind. I had learnt that it was out of the goodness of his heart that he tended the small patch of no-man's-land next to the nursing home, so that the residents, living out their final, frail years on earth, had something beautiful to enjoy.

The brusque giant had been immensely kind to me too, although it had taken me a while to understand this. In tending the small garden, the residents of the nursing home hadn't been his only focus of loving kindness. Several years ago I had woken to the same aroma that had caught my attention this morning. On that occasion, once again heeding my instincts, my paws had led me directly to the garden, where I'd discovered a cluster of plants with heart-shaped leaves and white flowers. I later discovered these plants were none other than catnip, planted for my personal enjoyment.

Today, as before, I wobbled up the few, stone steps from the pavement to the garden. I made my way across the lawn to the flower bed, where I once again found the source of the beguiling fragrance. I began chewing on the green stalks. Licking the flower stems and rubbing my face in the plants. Desire overwhelmed me. I began to quiver, before launching myself completely into the flower bed, crushing the stalks as I did and bringing the flowers down upon me.

I didn't care. In my unfettered craving for the heady fragrance, I stretched and curled and thoroughly immersed myself in the foliage and flowers of catnip, purring and rolling and thrilling in every last spine-tingling moment!

At some point, the scent became less vivid. As it always did. The effect began to wear off. Instead of rolling, I just lay there, dozing happily in a state of post-catnip afterglow.

I climbed out of the garden bed half an hour later, shaking off several bits of foliage which had stuck to me, before briefly grooming. It was only then that I glanced towards the nursing home and saw several residents sitting on cane chairs on the veranda. There was a group of six of them, beside a tea trolley. Further along the veranda, another two. I had noticed them sitting there on past occasions, but had never paid much attention. They would remain, silent and motionless as statues, save for the occasional lifting or lowering of a teacup. After the ecstatic joy I was in the habit of experiencing in the garden, followed by the post-catnip afterglow, it never seemed like there was much excitement to be had on the nursing home balcony.

What caught my attention today was not so much the residents themselves but what was behind them. Something I had never seen before—an open door!

It was of the sliding glass variety and in the past had always been firmly shut. Rest assured, dear reader, I had been up to investigate. On a number of past occasions, I had pressed my nose to that same glass pane, curious to see what lay behind the dark tint and curtains, but never to any avail. However, today there was a free entrance from the veranda to the inside. Could there be a more conspicuous invitation?

I made my way from the garden, up the gentle slope of a rockery, through a flowerbed. No sooner than I appeared from between a row of agapanthus plants, there was an unprecedented stirring of activity among the residents taking morning tea on the veranda.

"What a beautiful cat!" exclaimed one.

"Such markings!" observed another.

"Are those eyes really blue?" questioned a third.

Being The Most Beautiful Creature That Ever Lived, I am used to being admired to the point of being thoroughly bored by it. There are times I wish I could go out incognito, just another drab cat of indeterminate color, and walk down the street unnoticed. But no! Everywhere I go, I am besieged by attention.

Even so, when the residents, on what had been an entirely sedentary veranda, began to gesture and utter exclamations, I was taken aback for the simple reason that I didn't believe them to be capable of such things. I had also always thought of them collectively, as a single group, not one of them differentiated from another. But that morning I came to realize they were not only individuals, they had their own names. I paused on the veranda just long enough for one elderly woman I came to know as Rita to stroke me and pronounce my tail to be amazingly bushy, before heading to where I really wanted to go—inside.

It was a very large sitting room. Chairs and sofas lined the walls, interspersed with low tables, warm lamps, magazines and that day's newspapers. Softly lit, with tasteful paintings on the walls, what struck me most about the room was this: the ten people sitting in the chairs were like statues. They gave the appearance of being in one of those wax museums I'd heard about. Several heads were tilted against the back of the chairs. Others were slumped to the side. A couple were staring, unseeing, into mid-distance. All of them almost motionless.

Glancing around, surveying the scene, I noticed only one woman who seemed completely awake. Geeta was sitting alone and moving her mouth as though talking to someone—but not a sound escaped her lips.

It was Christopher, a large, elderly man with a shock of white hair, who was first to raise the alert. "It's a cat!" he exclaimed, as if the Queen of Sheba herself had just stepped into the room.

Christopher was sitting on his own, occupying most of a sofa. Given his enthusiastic tone, and because I didn't want to get kicked out of there before I'd had the chance to look around properly, I made my way over and hopped up beside him. He didn't hesitate to reach out and stroke me, chuckling as he did.

"Oh, this takes me back!" His voice was thick with feeling. "Our Jack died more than twenty years ago. This is the first cat

I've touched in all that time …"

I gazed up at him with my large, sapphire eyes, noticing the tears welling up in his own. His large hands, with their blotchy skin, were trembling. The jacket he was wearing, with its frayed cuffs, had evidently seen better days.

My usual impulse would have been to get away from him. But as he stroked me with such evident emotion, I found myself remembering Geshe-la's teachings from the previous Tuesday night. Which was how I found myself thinking: *May this act of kindness be a cause for me to attain complete and perfect enlightenment for the sake of all living beings.* A thought which, dear reader, instantly made me feel better about what was happening. I even sidled up to him and purred.

"Oh, she's an angel!" Christopher declared.

Others in the room were coming to, several of them beckoning to me with hand waves or calls of "Puss! Puss!" I rubbed myself up against Christopher's chest and arm, making sure to leave generous swathes of cream fur on his garments, before getting off the sofa and back onto the carpet.

Calls from other residents were more eager now, as was the gesturing. I made my way towards an alert-looking woman in a wheelchair, who was patting her lap. My jumps are not the most agile, on account of my rear legs, but any thoughts about my inelegance were nothing, compared to the rapture expressed by Yvette as she stroked me firmly. "Oh, just look at those eyes!" she crooned.

Other elderly women were getting up from their chairs and hobbling over. The heavily ringed hands of several people, along with stale breaths and a cloying, decidedly pharmaceutical aroma were not especially enjoyable. But, as with the old man, I recollected bodhicitta intention: *May this act of kindness be a cause for me to attain complete and perfect enlightenment for the sake of all living beings.* Once again, it made me feel better about being pawed and prodded amid the gathering buzz in the room.

There could be no doubting the excitement I was generating. One of the residents declared me to be the highlight of the day, before being quickly corrected by another—the week! Maybe even the month! The energy in the room had changed to one of engaged interest, delight and enthusiasm. No longer a wax museum, everyone wanted a part of me.

After Yvette in the wheelchair, I made my way to several others on a sofa. I decided to smooch every single resident in the room, on each occasion recollecting bodhicitta motivation. I remembered how Geshe-la had also advised that the more we repeat this intention, and the more it becomes ingrained in our thinking, then the more the mask becomes the person. Buddhist psychology. And as I repeated it now, I found myself wanting to do more. Wishing I could replicate myself to visit each one of them.

A legend goes that, when he was about to attain nirvana, Avalokiteshvara, the Buddha of Compassion, looked back and saw a rabbit in distress. He couldn't bear to leave the rabbit in pain. Telling Amitabha Buddha he had to return to help the rabbit, Amitabha observed that in samsara he'd find many other beings who were suffering. To help him in his compassionate efforts, Amitabha gave him a thousand hands and arms.

If only I'd had a thousand paws and a thousand bushy tails, right then!

Working my way around the room, I noticed a woman sitting in an alcove chair on her own. Breathing tubes were inserted in her nose. She looked pale and emaciated, with barely the energy to hold up her head. Her hands hung limply at her sides. But her gaze was fixed on me with warm interest.

Moving over to her chair, I jumped up onto the cushion beside her. She was wearing a light dressing-gown and her arms were like spindles. She had a shrunken appearance, the veins under the skin of her forehead clearly visible. But her expression changed and her smile transformed her features. She looked at me with the most heartfelt appreciation.

She lifted one of her arms and stroked me. I purred appreciatively, amping up the volume for her benefit while recollecting my bodhicitta motivation. I became aware of comments being made around the room.

"First time she's smiled in months," came one voice.

"I didn't think she could move her hands anymore," came another.

"She used to talk about her cats like they were her children," came a third.

This went on for some time, the noise level in the room continuing to climb, before another voice cut through the banter. A clear, more youthful voice of authority.

"So we have a visitor?" I glanced over to see a matronly-looking nurse in white uniform regarding me with no warmth whatsoever.

"Look at Hilda!" exclaimed a resident. "We didn't think she could move her arms anymore."

"I'm not sure having a cat at close quarters is such a good idea," the nurse stepped closer. "She needs help breathing as it is. What if she has an allergic reaction?"

"She's used to cats. Had them for years!" a voice quakily declared.

"She's loving it!" Christopher pointed out the obvious.

"But it's ... just off the streets!" said the nurse, gesturing at the open door. "For all we know, that cat is riddled with disease."

I turned to regard her with my most blue-blooded, imperious stare. Me? Disease? Did she have any idea who she was talking to?!

"You're a lively lot today!" came a different voice. A man's. He entered from the same corridor as the nurse and was wearing a stethoscope around his neck. He glanced over to where everyone else in the room was focused. "Oh, I see," he said.

"I'm assuming we need to get it out of here," said the nurse.

"Why assume that, Nurse Chapman?"

"Well ... asthma for one."

The man glanced around the room with a genial expression. "Anyone here allergic to cats?"

"I am!" declared the nurse.

"I was thinking of the residents. Primarily. I can prescribe antihistamine if needs be."

In the past I had encountered another person allergic to cats, who had made my life very difficult and had even tried to have me banned from The Himalaya Book Café. Fortunately, that distressing eventuality had never happened, thanks to the razor-sharp intelligence of Head Waiter Kusali. But it had made me extremely wary of cat-phobes.

"Hilda already has trouble breathing," pointed out the nurse.

"But look at the transformation," said the doctor.

Nurse Chapman tilted her head to one side. "Yes." She realized she wasn't winning anyone's support. "I suppose so."

"Pets can be wonderful therapy. You're all enjoying your visitor, aren't you?" he asked generally.

There was a chorus of enthusiasm.

Even though I hadn't spent much time on Hilda's chair, I could tell that I was wearying her. So I got off, headed across the room to the open door and, to groans of disappointment, made my exit as enigmatically and mercurially as I had arrived.

I returned to the nursing home, dear reader. Not that same day, nor even same week. But the following week, catching the unmistakable, alluring wafts of catnip from my windowsill and because it was a beautifully clear morning, I made my way to the garden where I enjoyed myself thoroughly before, once again, observing residents on the veranda.

The reaction, this second time, was much more rapid and enthusiastic. Before I'd fully emerged from the agapanthus, a beady-eyed man had called out with enthusiasm, "She's back!" He pointed, "Over there!"

Within moments I was being beckoned by everyone seated outside. I sashayed towards them, rubbing each resident around the legs luxuriantly, while recalling bodhicitta motivation. As I did, I was aware of a flurry of activity within, as people in the sitting room pulled themselves up in their armchairs, preparing to come outside.

I saved them the bother. Of all the residents, there was one I especially wanted to revisit—and she wasn't on the veranda. I made my way through the open door and glanced around, taking in the bright smiles and waving arms, the raised voices and entreaties.

She was sitting exactly where she'd been before, motionless and apparently unable to speak, but looking at me with just the same warm affection. I made my way directly to her.

"Oh, Hilda's the lucky one!" cried Yvette, but without any trace of rancor, as though secretly pleased by the direction I was taking.

"Just like last time," called another.

"Although she did spread her affections around," observed a third.

"Who? Hilda?" asked a man with faux innocence.

"Cheeky devil, Christopher!" responded someone else.

The lounge of the nursing home was positively abuzz with repartee as I leapt up to be with Hilda, purring appreciatively as she began to stroke me. I headbutted her gently at the heart before gazing up into her eyes, sensing how deeply she missed this contact with a cat, and how very much she appreciated my presence. All the while recollecting my bodhicitta motivation.

I continued on my rounds, recognizing some of the residents by the touch of a fabric, the clank of a bracelet, the expression on a face; once again I experienced each one of them as an individual, rather than a collective group. As I felt how each one of **them** felt having me on a lap, rubbing against an arm, listening to me purr, I realized how much happiness I was giving. And as I did all that, dear reader, I found myself feeling deeply happy myself. Not the irresistible, salivating, spine-tingling happiness of catnip. A different kind of happiness. The sense of profound wellbeing that comes from what you give, rather than from what you receive. From connecting to the hearts and minds of others with love.

Not everyone in the establishment was ready to connect in such a way, however. At least, not yet. I observed Nurse Chapman arrive to find what all the clamor was about. Glancing in my direction, she soon got her answer. And while she made no attempt to disturb where I was kneading the generous lap of a woman in a wheelchair, she did not look exactly thrilled to see me.

It was when I made my way towards Christopher, who seemed somewhat younger than the others, that the dynamics changed. The so-called 'cheeky devil' had a mischievous look in his eye. Stepping directly onto his knees, I noticed tiny flecks of color on his corduroy trousers. His fingers had a strong and not unlikeable aroma which I soon recognized. Oil paint.

The nurse went to check on the residents on the veranda. Conversation in the room continued to be lively, and a few moments later another woman appeared. Jolly looking, but with an air of control, she stepped into the room and quickly noticed who was causing all the excitement. She came over in my direction.

"So you're the one I've heard so much about!" she exclaimed, lowering herself to her haunches and reaching over to stroke me. "A real beauty. Must be a pedigree of some sort," she observed.

Over her shoulder I saw that the nurse had returned and was looking in our direction.

"She's certainly livened things up around here. I don't think I've ever seen the residents so engaged!"

"Well, it was Nurse Chapman who found her for us," Christopher looked up at the nurse with a glint in his eye. "I believe she is what's known as a Therapy Cat."

"Great idea, Claire!" the woman glanced over at the nurse. "What a wonderful innovation. I do hope we'll be seeing more of this feline visitor."

Nurse Chapman was only too happy to take credit for this unexpected turn of events. "Of course," said she. "We'll be encouraging her."

It was several weeks later when I was back on my sill, as the Dalai Lama went through his end-of-day briefing with Tenzin and Oliver.

"Anything else to report?" asked His Holiness, after official business had been discussed.

As the three men leaned back in their chairs, Oliver said with a twinkle, "Well, there **is** something involving an important household member."

"Oh, yes?" a playful expression appeared on the Dalai Lama's face.

"I bumped into Marianne Ponter in town a few days ago—you know, she runs the aged care home along the road?" he tilted his head in that direction.

"Yes, yes."

"She was telling me about a breakthrough they've had with their residents. For years, they've been trying to come up with ways to engage their interest. To promote conversation and activity."

"Keep young?" offered His Holiness.

"Exactly," nodded Oliver. "They've tried board games, computer games, outings, tai chi. Apparently the most effective, by far, has been visits from a Therapy Cat."

Both the Dalai Lama and Tenzin looked puzzled.

"Best practice these days in aged care facilities, apparently. It seems that when residents are able to play with cats or dogs, the whole place comes alive."

Both His Holiness and Tenzin were nodding. "When we are with pets," observed the Dalai Lama. "We can be ourselves. No need to pretend."

"They take us back to our childhood," suggested Tenzin.

"According to Marianne, the Therapy Cat that visits them is particularly beautiful. Apparently she has big blue eyes and a charcoal face and she walks with a limp."

All three men turned to look in my direction.

"Marianne says she is very good with the residents, especially the frail ones. There's a lady in there who has hardly moved for weeks, but she is able to muster the energy to stroke the Therapy Cat."

"Therapy Cat," His Holiness used the title for the very first time, as he gazed at me. "Easier, for us Buddhists, just to say bodhi**catt**va!"

The men laughed.

"I am pleased she is offering love and compassion," the Dalai Lama continued. "Motivated by bodhicitta, this is one of the most important elements of our practice, is it not?"

"One of the four you mentioned," Oliver reminded him of their previous conversation.

"Oh yes," agreed His Holiness, smiling. "The four paws of spiritual success."

Some minutes later, when his Executive Assistants had left, His Holiness came over to me at the sill and we shared a few moments of silent communion together. There was no need for him to congratulate me for my enlightened behavior. Or to encourage me to do more. I had discovered for myself that the sense of wellbeing that arises from practicing bodhicitta, albeit in my wonky-legged way, was profoundly heartwarming. Even when begun with contrived intention, with the thought to 'fake it till you make it', the results were so strong that I could feel them. Why would I wish to stop?

The only thing the Dalai Lama said before he got up was, "The second aspect we are reminded of whenever we see a Buddha ..." He was glancing over at the wall-hanging of

Shakyamuni Buddha. "Are you looking, my little Snow Lion?"

I was looking, as it happened. Looking very hard for the four aspects. But still, I couldn't see.

The very next morning I paid another visit to the nursing home. This time I didn't even pause at the catnip. I ventured directly across the garden, up the rockery, through the agapanthus and onto the veranda. There I was greeted as a much-loved friend. And moving indoors, I went first of all to Hilda. While I was sitting on the arm of her chair, she stroked me and quite audibly said the word 'darling'.

To say that the whole room rippled with excitement at this utterance would be no exaggeration, dear reader. It was the first word Hilda had spoken in more than two years!

By the time I left, I was in the very best of spirits. Not only because I was applying the second paw of spiritual success to my own life; also because of what I anticipated next.

Instead of returning to Namgyal, I turned in the opposite direction, continuing up the road well past the point where it became more suburban. Tall pine trees formed an avenue on either side of the road. Lush green verges carpeted either side. Driveways led from the road toward houses that were set so far back, you couldn't see more than a gable here, a rooftop there.

Number 21 Tara Crescent had become one of my favorite places in the whole world to visit, and as I reached it, I turned directly into the driveway. This was the home of Serena, her husband Sid, and Sid's child by his first marriage, Zahra.

I'd overheard recent snippets from both Mrs. Trinci and Serena in the kitchen downstairs about end-of-term arrangements, and that Zahra had been due to return from boarding school two days before. But even if I hadn't been privy to such conversations, I told myself, I would still have sensed it. My feline intuition would have sensed a change. A shift in energy up the road. A magnetic attraction towards the house I had first visited when it was undergoing major renovations, prior to Sid and Serena moving in.

At a bend in the driveway, I caught my first glimpse of the house in several months. It was a raised, rambling bungalow with a spacious wraparound veranda. What always caught my immediate attention was a tower rising from the north wing of the house, stretching up two floors and shrouded with ivy. At its top was a room with large, picture windows on all four sides.

I thought of it as Zahra's and my room—the perfect viewing platform from which to observe the sun, the moon, the stars and the snow-capped Himalayas. It was a place where we'd lounge together, enjoying each other's company, no matter what time of day or season of the year. It was a room from which we could not only survey the surrounding countryside, like devas from the realms above, but also take in the scent of Himalaya pine through the open window. The fragrances of forest flowers and the distant sound of bells and chanting, wafting up from Namgyal Monastery, had always imbued this place with a special feeling. I could hardly wait to return there to be with Zahra today.

Half way up the driveway I heard the distinctive sound of her laughter coming from inside the house. My paw steps quickened. Our reunions, after her return from school, were always joyful occasions. So looking forward to seeing her, I made my way along the lawn at the side of the gravel driveway.

With no thought except for what I imagined lay ahead, I was only a short distance from the downstairs veranda when I looked up and saw him. The ferocious tabby who had attacked me several weeks earlier, near Mr. Patel's stall! That large, muscular body was instantly recognizable. I couldn't see his face, because he was curled up in the sunshine. Dozing, slap bang in the middle of the veranda table. Like he lived there.

CHAPTER FOUR

I PAUSED, TAKING IN THE SCENE, SCARCELY ABLE TO BELIEVE what I was seeing. The tabby was luxuriating in the warmth of the morning, front paws draped over the side of the wooden table and eyes shut, looking for all the world like the household puss. Lord of the manor. King of the castle.

Just how long I remained there, frozen and transfixed, I cannot say. I knew the ferocious beast could blink open his eyes at any moment. That if he did, he'd be sure to see me. And he'd almost certainly give chase.

At the same time, part of me was hoping that something would happen to change the status quo. In particular, that Zahra would make an appearance and somehow bring this hideous aberration to an end.

Suddenly, there was a terrifying thud on the grass beside me. A clod of earth! A hundred flecks exploded right beside me. No sooner was I aware of this than another missile landed, narrowly missing my paw.

I looked up. A uniformed gardener was on the other side of the lawn, drawing back his arm. Preparing to hurl yet another clod. And he was aiming straight at me!

Instinct took over. I about-turned, scampering in retreat. A direct hit would be agonizing. With my rear legs being so frail, I would probably be knocked over—or knocked out.

Another lump of earth exploded directly behind me. I scrambled faster than I had in my life, running more quickly than I thought possible. In those crazy, heart-palpitating moments there was no time and no thought—only fear and the desperate need to escape.

The gardener didn't seem to be chasing me. The further I got away, the fewer the projectiles. Nearing the bend in the driveway where the house disappeared from view, I glanced back for the first time. The gardener was standing in the same place, arm drawn back to launch another projectile in my direction.

The tabby, I couldn't fail to notice, was now sitting upright on the veranda table, watching me closely. Observing my retreat through those baleful, yellow eyes.

Still hastening, I reached the road, scurrying beneath the avenue of pines, still acting on instinct more than reason, until I realized I was no longer under threat.

My pace slowed down, but I was still moving much faster than usual. Agitated and confused, I had no idea where I was heading or what I was going to do next. The appalling discovery

I had just made at 21 Tara Crescent had thrown me. Spooked and bewildered, I was an altogether very discombobulated cat.

I continued along the road until I reached the garden next to the nursing home, then the fence of Namgyal Monastery. In no mood to settle, adrenalin still pumping through my system, I carried on down the hill, more from pure instinct than from any plan.

Being lunchtime, it was probably habit that drew me down the hill and past the market stalls, to the place where I was used to losing myself in a convivial buzz, nourished by morsels of whatever had been that day's *plat du jour*. I am referring, of course, to The Himalaya Book Café.

The restaurant was in full swing when I arrived. Almost all the tables were occupied and lunch was being served. Still distracted, I made my way through the brass-handled swing doors. To the right, the café was all wicker chairs and white tablecloths, walls resplendent with brocaded Tibetan thangkas. To the left, up a few steps behind an ornate, teak, reception counter, was the well-stocked bookstore. Underneath the reception counter, dozing in their baskets were Franc's two loyal canines, Marcel the Frenchie and Kyi Kyi the Lhasa Apso. Exchanging greetings, the moment our wet noses touched I was brought back to the present, to the here and now, away from the trauma of what I'd just been through.

I made my way to the magazine rack, near the bottom of the steps which led to the bookstore. Through force of habit I climbed to the top shelf where I was wont to appear, resplendent between the covers of *Vogue* and *Vanity Fair*. This was my vantage point in the café, the place from where I'd observed the goings-on for the past seven years, and where I had been photographed by countless tourists. Usually a place of sanctuary and pleasure, one where I enjoyed being greatly admired, I found it hard to settle that day. With the immediate danger behind me, what followed was a bitter realization: I was no longer welcome at 21 Tara Crescent.

Serena and Sid had adopted the tabby, or at least allowed him to move in. And, it seemed to me, they had instructed their staff to chase away other cats. So much for the special connection I had always felt with all three of them. The connection I'd believed was fully reciprocated.

I hadn't heard Serena say anything about the new feline in their lives. But I wasn't privy to every conversation she had. Did this mean I would never be able to return to the beautiful home with the tower between the sun, the moon, the mountains and the stars? Would I never again spend time with Zahra, just the two of us in each other's presence, not needing to do anything in particular but feel the easy warmth of our indefinable connection?

As I came out of my state of shock, it was replaced by a feeling of hollowness. Of loss. One which could have made me very unhappy indeed had it not been for the arrival of Head Waiter Kusali, efficient as ever, who swept up to the magazine rack with a small saucer of fish in cheese sauce—the contents of today's fish pie. Deliciously tangy and creamy, as I caught a waft I found that I was suddenly very hungry indeed. All sad thoughts were banished, as I sank my head towards the saucer and mashed away with gusto.

We cats enjoy mouse-sized meals several times throughout the day. I have to confess that the portions at The Himalaya Book Café were usually somewhat more than mouse-sized, more approaching the proportions of an especially plump rat. Which was why, after my postprandial grooming session, as well as fatigue from my over exertions of that morning, I was overcome by a familiar feeling of being pleasantly replete. Very definitely in the mood for a siesta. I lay down, paws neatly beneath me, before relaxing into what Ludo may have termed 'croissant pose'. And so, to sleep.

When I woke up mid-afternoon, the café had fallen into its usual post-lunch lull. I was instantly aware of a conversation happening in the seating area just behind me. Two sofas and a coffee table in the bookstore offered a good view of both the bookstore and restaurant. This afternoon I heard the voices of Franc, Bronnie (Sam's wife), and Angie (Sam's new bookstore assistant). And it was their mention of the name 'Mrs. Williams' that grabbed my attention.

Even though Mrs. Williams had never stepped foot inside The Himalaya Book Café, hers had become a name of great notoriety in recent weeks. It had started when Sam and Bronnie moved apartments. They had been looking for something with two bedrooms, so they could put up family and friends visiting from home. Like most young couples, their challenge was money. So when they found an airy, first-floor apartment which not only boasted two large bedrooms, but also a view of the Himalayas from the lounge window, and all within their very modest budget, they could hardly believe their good fortune. They certainly didn't question the low rent. On the contrary, they couldn't wait to sign the twelve-month lease.

They knew nothing about the occupant of the ground-floor apartment. When they'd been shown through by the real estate agent, they'd caught a glimpse of a tall, young man heading into the front door from the shared, ground-floor hallway. They had assumed he lived there alone, or perhaps with a friend or partner. Not that they gave the matter a moment's thought. Why would they? In their minds, they were already arranging their furniture in the wonderful new flat. Planning which bedroom they'd make their own. Picturing evenings eating delicious meals by the open, picture window, while the sun set over the resplendent Himalayas.

The day they moved in had been an exhausting saga involving multiple journeys, much heavy lifting and frayed nerves. Collapsing onto the unmade bed in their new apartment—who knew which packing case they'd stored their linen in—they had been woken by a pungent stench that seemed to be coming from their kitchen. It wasn't, in fact. The downstairs neighbor, Mrs. Williams, was fond of smoked kippers. Her kitchen was directly under theirs. And as they were soon to discover, there was nothing insulating them from the odors or noises that she produced downstairs. Whatever Mrs. Williams emitted filled their apartment too. The only way to avoid the choking miasma was to leave home. Which they duly did—coming in for breakfast at The Himalaya Book Café before starting work.

Arriving home from work at the end of their first day in the new apartment, Sam from the bookstore and Bronnie from the children's literacy program where she worked, they couldn't open the front door into the shared hallway. Or at least, not fully. During the day, it turned out, the hallway had been jammed full of old furniture and other items—two ancient bicycles, a plaster birdbath, a rusted bed leaning vertically against the wall, plus boxes and boxes of anonymous, plastic-wrapped items. The shared front door wouldn't fully open. Only the narrowest path remained to the back of the hall and the door to the ground-floor flat and, coincidentally, to the stairs that led up to their apartment.

Bronnie and Sam had arrived home separately and reached the same, independent conclusion: their downstairs neighbors were on the move. Perhaps that meant their smoked kipper experience would be a one-off? Would a new downstairs neighbor present less of an olfactory challenge?

Bronnie had wanted to make their first dinner in their new home special. She had set their small kitchen table with flowers and lit two tea lights. Sam put something soft and jazzy on the sound system to create a romantic ambiance, then poured them each a glass of wine. They worked together in the kitchen on one of their favorite stir-fries and had just sat down to eat when the arguing began. An elderly woman's voice erupted volcanically, countered in the next moment by a young man's. Suddenly, Bronnie and Sam found themselves caught in the midst of outraged dispute.

Exactly what the row was about was unclear—while the voices were loud, the diction was muffled. If Sam and Bronnie had opened their own front door they would have been able to hear it, as clearly as if they had been in the same room. But they had no interest in prying.

Besides, the argument was suddenly escalating, threatening to turn violent. The woman was screaming at the man, calling him a 'good-for-nothing'. He was roaring at her for being an 'ungrateful bitch', with a variety of expletives thrown in. Their voices rose uncontrollably.

Meeting Bronnie's anxious eyes across the table, Sam started to say, "D'you think I need to …" at the same time as Bronnie said, "You'd better go down."

Pushing his seat back from the table, Sam started to make his way to the door when the quarreling suddenly stopped. The two of them continued their meal in subdued silence.

It turned out that Sam and Bronnie had moved in above the neighbors from hell. Within days it became clear that, despite the build-up of bric-a-brac in the hallway, Mrs. Williams and her son Barry weren't going anywhere. Much worse, they were hoarders. The miscellany of items in the hallway grew by the day, new items in bags and boxes being jammed in the midst of the larger ones. When Sam, on first meeting Barry Williams outside the front door, remarked with concern about the hazard these items presented should either of them have a fire in their apartment, he was told to mind his own business. Only not as politely as that.

The kippers turned out to be a three or four times a week event, smoking Sam and Bronnie out of their home on every occasion. And the rows continued with the same frequency—a form of sport, it seemed, between Mrs. Williams and her belligerent son, especially once they had some alcohol in them. Once, when the rowing continued late into the night, Sam felt obliged to go downstairs, knock on the door, and ask them to keep the noise down. While this had the desired effect, he returned home next day to find a seven-page spiteful letter stuffed under his door, ranting about freedom of expression, the right to lively discussion, and page after page about the degenerate, rebel colony of America.

Naturally, Sam and Bronnie appealed to their rental agent. Who wasn't much interested. He reminded them what a bargain rent they were paying for such a large apartment with mountain views. Plus the fact that breaking the lease on their agreement would mean they were personally liable for the first six months' rent, whether they lived in the apartment or not. When they sent photos of the jammed-up hallway and pointed out the fire hazard that it presented, someone somewhere must have persuaded Mrs Williams to find a home for her junk collection—but only for a while. The thinning out of items in the hallway was only temporary.

Sam and Bronnie were reaching the end of their tether. They couldn't afford to give up six months' rent for a property they weren't going to live in. But they'd also started to dread going home each evening. It didn't help when another neighbor told them that their house was notorious up and down the street. The upstairs apartment had been empty for over six months, on account of its reputation. Prior to that, no tenants had stayed for more than a few weeks. One female occupant had left after just two nights.

Bronnie had taken to stopping off at The Himalaya Book Café on her way home from work in the late afternoon. Taking up a position on the back-of-house banquette near the magazine rack, she would order a drink and wait till Sam had finished his duties as bookstore manager—duties which appeared never-ending, and which he seemed to extend later and later, delaying the inevitable moment when they'd have to make their way home.

It was on such an occasion that Geshe Wangpo made one of his rare appearances at The Himalaya Book Café. The formidable lama had a very busy teaching schedule as well as many administrative responsibilities, which left him with little spare time. But his visits to the café were not unprecedented. And through the years, whenever he made what seemed to be a social visit, his manifestation turned out to be pivotal in light of what followed.

Bronnie and Sam had been sitting on the banquette, together but apart, as they scrolled distractedly through their social media feeds. Glancing up, they found themselves in the presence of Geshe Wangpo.

Out of respect, they scrambled to their feet; the lama gestured for them to sit.

They invited him to join them and he slid onto the bench seat opposite. Never one for small talk or chit chat, it didn't take Geshe Wangpo long to find out why the two of them were sitting in the semi-darkness, staring at their mobile devices, instead of taking in the panoramic vista of the Himalaya mountains from their new apartment.

They told him about the Williams mother and son. The fighting and unpleasantness. The odors and the clutter. The expectation that they'd open the front door of their apartment one day and be unable to make their way out to the street.

"We can't afford to move out," Sam summarized their dilemma. "But our life there is just ..." he was shaking his head.

"We want to do the right thing," chimed Bronnie. "But what is the right thing, in such circumstances? Should we involve the police next time they fight? Go the legal route?"

"As students trying to practice bodhicitta," rejoined Sam, with his own more cerebral questions. "Should we just roll over and accept it?" He shrugged, a hopeless expression on his face. "If you want to practice compassion and loving kindness, does the Dharma say you should let people do whatever they like? Does bodhicitta mean you have to be a doormat?"

Geshe Wangpo fixed Sam and Bronnie with an expression of such forceful command that they immediately stopped talking.

"No doormats!" Although his voice was calm, his tone was emphatic. "No idiot compassion."

Opposite him, Sam and Bronnie regarded him, transfixed, before Sam asked, "Idiot compassion?"

Geshe Wangpo leaned forward in his seat and said simply, "Compassion without wisdom." Settling back against his seat, he gave them a few moments to absorb what he'd just told them, before continuing. "The wall-hanging of Lama Tsong Khapa in our temple, the one with the yellow hat, you remember it?"

"Yes," Sam was well-versed on such details. "With his two disciples, Gyaltsab Je and Khedrub Je."

"Very good," Geshe Wangpo nodded. "Do you know what quality Lama Tsong Khapa symbolizes?"

"Wisdom?" ventured Sam.

"And his two disciples?"

Here, Sam shook his head.

"They represent the qualities of compassion and power," the lama told him. "Always, these three go together. Compassion, wisdom, power. When you have compassion and power but no wisdom, this is idiot compassion. Compassion and wisdom but no power—what can you achieve?" he shrugged. "All three are necessary, together."

Furrows had appeared on Sam's forehead as he processed the implications of this. "What I'm struggling to understand," he spoke after a while, "is how this applies to my neighbor."

Geshe-la pursed his lips. "Right now," he regarded Sam and Bronnie evenly, "you have little power. Little influence. When you do—and things can change, especially between neighbors— then you must use your power with wisdom and compassion."

He leaned back against the banquette.

"So until then," Bronnie prompted. "Are you saying the situation's hopeless?"

The lama regarded her with a gentle smile. "Until then ..." he said, "take special care of your Precious Treasure."

Both of them looked bewildered.

"The important thing about a Precious Treasure is to recognize the person as such. How many of your friends offer you the opportunity to practice patience that Mrs. Williams does?"

They were shaking their heads.

"How many of your nearest and dearest test your ability to retain your equanimity like her?"

A droll smile appeared on Sam's face. Bronnie just looked miserable.

"There are few people in our lives like Mrs. Williams. When we encounter them, if we are wise, we try to reframe the experience. To see the opportunities they provide."

"I was hoping you could perform some miracle to change the way she is," said Bronnie.

"What miracle?" asked Geshe Wangpo.

"I don't know," Bronnie was shaking her head. "Make her migrate to Australia. Disappear in a puff of smoke."

Geshe Wangpo acknowledged the humor in her suggestion with a twinkle. "Puff of smoke," he nodded, smiling. "That would be a miracle. Sometimes people say they want lamas to do other miracles like mind reading, telling the future and so forth. But these are small miracles. Not so important. Changing your heart, **that** is a much bigger miracle. Only you can make it happen," he said. "And I think you already know how from my class," he gestured in the direction of Namgyal Monastery, "how to practice *tong-len*—the form of compassion-based meditation, where you visualize taking away someone's suffering and giving them happiness."

"Take away Mrs. Williams suffering?" queried Bronnie, wrinkling her nose.

"Give **her** happiness?" Sam was aghast.

Geshe Wangpo was nodding.

"But she's such a deeply unlikeable person," said Sam.

"Which is what makes her such a Precious Treasure. Who doesn't find it easy to wish for the happiness of their friends? Or to visualize taking suffering away from their loved ones? Such things are easy. Even criminals love their friends. Thieves, murderers—even they have no problem helping those they care about. That requires no inner development at all.

"But true bodhicitta cannot be partial or biased. We do not wish for the happiness of only some but not others. So you see, cultivating equanimity is vital. And to do that, we need to practice on one such as Mrs. Williams."

There was a pause before Bronnie, shaking her head, admitted, "I have to be honest, Geshe-la. I don't think I could bring myself to do it. The number of nights at home she and her son have ruined! The stress of living with those blow-ups! And you never know when it's going to happen next."

"Yes, yes," he reached out, squeezing her hand briefly in consolation. "But imagine if you could take away her suffering and its true causes. Her bad relationship with her son. Her attachment to junk. Her self-centered way of living. Just imagine if you could give her happiness and its true causes. Loving kindness towards others—including her neighbors. Non-attachment to old bicycles and birdbaths. What kind of neighbor would that make her?"

"The ideal neighbor," said Bronnie.

"You see," shrugged Geshe Wangpo. "Not so difficult. Mrs. Williams is a person in pain. She is one who suffers. And who probably doesn't have any tools to deal with her suffering. But you do. You know how to bring the suffering she gives you to your own practice, to use it to fuel your own inner growth."

Sam and Bronnie digested his words in silence for a while, before Sam asked, "If we practice tong-len, focusing on Mrs. Williams, could that, like, change the energy in the house?

"You are asking if it will stop her fighting with her son or cooking kippers?" Geshe Wangpo was a straight talker.

Sam moved his chin from side to side. "I s'pose."

"Perhaps," replied the lama. "Perhaps not." Then leaning back against his seat he fixed them both with a level gaze. "You are both intelligent young people. Educated. You know that the experience of an event depends on the mind of the experiencer, even more than the event itself."

They nodded.

"I'm showing you a way to change your experience, by changing your mind."

That encounter had happened over a month ago. Since then, I'd overheard regular updates on the Mrs. Williams' situation. In the days that followed Sam and Bronnie's encounter with Geshe Wangpo, things on the home front improved dramatically. No violent arguments. Few fried kippers. They wondered if their tong-len practice was taking effect.

But an especially bad week of rows had culminated in the worst one of all, which only ended when Barry Williams stormed out of the house, slamming the front door so hard that the towers of junk in the hall came tumbling down. It had taken Sam and Bronnie more than twenty minutes to clear a pathway, just so that they could get out of the house next morning.

While the tong-len practice performed no overnight miracles, Sam reported a change nonetheless. Frustrating as things continued to be, somehow the meditation practice helped take the sting out of things. There were still wrangling, raised voices. The inescapable miasma of fried, smoked fish. The sideways shuffle to get to the front door. But Sam and Bronnie felt less animosity, less agitation. Recognizing how miserable it must be to be Mrs. Williams, they even found themselves feeling sorry for her on occasion.

Hearing her name invoked that afternoon, I wondered if there had been any developments. Rising from the magazine rack, I made my way up the steps to the bookstore, hopping onto the sofa next to Franc. Facing him were Bronnie and the new bookstore assistant, Angela—an athletic, young redhead from Bronnie's hometown of Vancouver, whose pale skin colored whenever when she felt emotional. Marcel and Kyi Kyi dozed under the table, and Franc reached out to stroke my neck as their conversation continued.

"For the past two days," Bronnie was saying, "it's been completely quiet. We think she must have gone away."

"And the son?" asked Franc.

"We don't think he lives there. He seems to visit about three times a week."

"Which is when they row?" asked Franc.

Bronnie nodded.

"Maybe she's gone on holiday?" suggested Angela hopefully, putting down the book she had been studying on forest hiking in Northern India.

"A long one, home to England to stay with relatives," said Franc.

"Involving a lengthy sea journey," Angela giggled.

"On a ship that sinks," offered Franc.

"Oh Franc!" Angela's neck erupted in a rash of pink blotches. "That doesn't sound like enlightened speech to me."

"I'm afraid it isn't," he met her gaze with a weary expression. "But I'm a Buddhist, not a Buddha. As you will discover the longer you work here."

At that moment, Sam appeared at the entrance, carrying a colorful display of tulips in a wicker basket.

"These aren't for you," he called to Bronnie, as he walked to where we were sitting. He placed the basket on the table, before sitting next to me. "I was just about to leave home when the doorbell rang. Delivery for Mrs. Williams," he nodded towards the flowers.

Bronnie looked surprised. "Why bring them here?"

"Look at the note," he gestured.

On a card stuck into the floral display was a handwritten message which Bronnie read aloud: "Sorry to hear about your fall. I hope your leg heals quickly and you're up and about soon.

Love, Millie."

Bronnie's expression was quizzical. "I'm still not getting it?"

Everyone was looking to Sam for an explanation.

"Well, she's not at home," he said. "And it seems like she hasn't been for a few days. From this, I'm guessing she's in hospital." He tilted his chin in the direction of the local health center. "Remember how Geshe Wangpo said that you need power, wisdom and compassion to make an impact? And we didn't have any power—back then. But that things can change?"

Bronnie was nodding, even though she still seemed confused.

"Well, perhaps this is the change we need," Sam continued. "I was thinking, I could deliver them to her in hospital."

They all focused on the basket of tulips—mostly shades of pink and purple, with two red blossoms in the middle.

"You mean, like a circuit-breaker?" The penny dropped for Bronnie.

"Exactly," said Sam.

"It would be a nice surprise for her," observed Angela.

"The last thing she'd expect a neighbor to do," observed Franc.

"The last thing I would have thought about doing," agreed Sam, "if it hadn't been for Geshe Wangpo. But I'm guessing it's worth a try."

That afternoon, I left The Himalaya Book Café in a state of maximum vigilance. Although the trip home to Namgyal was short and very familiar, that morning's upsetting discovery of the tabby at 21 Tara Crescent had put me on edge. Even though I had been threatened by him only once, seeing him again, having taking occupation of my much-loved haunt, made me very aware of him. It seemed that he was no longer just a passing tomcat but a constant, threatening presence. A malevolent being that might emerge from behind a wall or doorway at any moment. And who knew what would happen if there wasn't someone around to help?

Hyper-aware all the way home, I headed through the late afternoon crowd, my whiskers tuned to full alert. I made sure there was a wide margin of ground he'd need to cross to get to me. And plenty of people to stop him. And was it my imagination, or were there a pair of menacing, tabby eyes watching me, as I arrived at Namgyal Monastery and made my way to the downstairs window left open specially for my use?

In the evening I settled on my sill overlooking Namgyal Courtyard. The windows of the monks' quarters were glowing like orange panels in the darkness; an early summer breeze was catching wisps of Nag Champa incense and carrying it high, high above the golden roof of the temple and up into a night sky sprinkled with stars.

This was one of my favorite times of all, when it was just the two of us, His Holiness and me, alone in the evening, free from interruptions. He was sitting at his desk, studying a book. I sat contemplating the day's events.

With the passage of time, I was feeling less shaken up by what had happened at 21 Tara Crescent, but it was hard to avoid the hollow feeling that my special place in that household seemed to have been taken over by the tabby. Mulling over how very suddenly happy domesticity could turn into a horror show, I was also remembering what had happened to Sam and Bronnie, and their battles with Mrs Williams.

For the first time, a decidedly uncomfortable idea occurred to me. One that had escaped me before but which, once recognized, was impossible to dismiss. Could it be that Geshe Wangpo's advice might apply to me too?

Was I supposed to change my experience of reality by transforming my mind? Was I expected to see that tabby as a 'Precious Treasure'? It was easy to see how this could apply to Mrs Williams, in the case of Sam and Bronnie. Of course they should do it. But me and the tabby? Should I really be wishing for the happiness of that savage beast—the one who had usurped me in the affections of others? Was I capable of it? Did I even want to?

I was contemplating this most displeasing notion, when the Dalai Lama turned from his seat to face me directly. "I've always loved these verses," he told me. I saw that he was reading from his very well-thumbed copy of Shantideva's *Guide to the Bodhisattva's Way of Life*. He continued:

"If the thought to relieve
Living creatures of merely a headache
Is a beneficial intention
Endowed with infinite goodness,
Then what need is there to mention
The wish to dispel their inconceivable misery,

Wishing every single one of them
To realize boundless good qualities?
The intention to benefit all beings
Which does not arise in others even for their own sake,
Is an extraordinary jewel of the mind,
And its birth is an unprecedented wonder."

As was so often the case, His Holiness just happened to be giving voice to a subject that spoke directly to what someone in his presence was thinking about. In this case, that someone was me. And 'wishing every single one of them' had a very specific connotation.

"Don't you love that phrase "jewel of the mind", my little Snow Lion?" he asked, moving from his desk to sit next to me. "It can be very challenging to practice bodhicitta with true equanimity. Perhaps we want all beings to be happy—except for one or two. But those one or two ... perhaps they are special cases. Perhaps they are the ones who can help us polish that extraordinary jewel of the mind. To make it into a thing of great beauty."

As he reached out to stroke me, I was caught up in the most curious sensation. I was touched by the benevolence that accompanied His Holiness wherever he went, and that pervaded the minds of all he was with. But this time the sensation was somehow different. It was as though I was being subtly lifted to a new perspective, one that didn't seem at all far from the one I usually occupied, but was a vantage of lucid objectivity. One where I was no longer His Holiness' Cat—or any separate mind at all—but instead enjoyed a state of panoramic consciousness, viewing everything from a place of loving kindness.

In this state, I only needed to think of a place or being, and I was there. Because of what had happened earlier that day, when I recollected the tabby, I saw what appeared as a small, vulnerable creature, just like any other feline, seeking the safety of a home and regular meals, wishing to belong, to give and receive love. And as I perceived this, I had no feelings that any of these should be withheld from him. What reason could there be for wishing the wellbeing of one feline, but not another? Why should he be denied contentment?

Turning my thoughts to Mrs. Williams, I perceived an old woman battling with impulses as self-destructive as they were ruinous to others. Someone who lived in isolation, in a world which would become smaller and smaller with time, all the while deepening the grooves of her own negativity.

Everywhere, it was easy to recognize, were beings with needs. Beings seeking happiness and fulfillment, some wisely, others in ways that could only prove disastrous. And in my state of benevolent objectivity, one so expansive that it seemed to contain everything in the heavens and below—the tabby, Mrs. Williams, the whole of Dharamshala and everywhere in the universe beyond—there was no seeking to control or to manage. No will to order what could not be ordered, or command what could not be commanded. Instead, there was only the playing out of appearances, a ceaseless, celestial dance held in a mind that was luminous with loving kindness.

Just as swiftly as I had been lifted into this state, I seemed to slip back again to being HHC. Although as I did so, I realized that the Dalai Lama had offered me a gift. A glimpse, perhaps, suggesting how he perceived reality all the time? An unexpected lifting of the veil of subjectivity at a time he felt I needed it?

"Bodhicitta sounds very nice," His Holiness told me softly. "Wishing all beings to have boundless good qualities, these are sweet-sounding words. But, I think, not easy. To some extent bodhicitta, the second principle, depends on renunciation, the first. It is only if we can turn away from hatred and attachment—only by not favoring this one or being partial to that one—that we can be authentic in wishing for the full enlightenment of **every** living being without exception."

The following week, I was in my usual afternoon spot at The Himalaya Book Café. There was a lull at the café, one of its few occupants being the young man from Europe who had asked Geshe Wangpo at his class, "Who am I to become enlightened?" In recent days he had been a frequent visitor to the café, sitting in the corner with his laptop, seeming disengaged when he was looking at it, and gloomy when he was not.

Next thing I knew, Franc was bounding up the steps beside the magazine rack. He'd been away for a few days in Delhi and, seeing Sam rearranging stock on the bookshelves, was eager for an update on Mrs. Williams.

Sam explained how getting the flowers to her hadn't been quite as straightforward as he had hoped. He had visited the main hospital to discover that she hadn't been admitted there. It was only after asking around and phone calls that he'd tracked her down to a clinic attached to a nursing home on the other side of town. A sprawling place with a confusing layout, so finding her ward number had also been something of a mission.

"She was completely charmless when I arrived," reported Sam, as the two of them stood at the bookstore entrance. "No thanks for bringing in the flowers just, "You can put them there!" Anyway, her leg was in plaster. I said I was sorry to hear about the fall. Turns out a suitcase fell on top of her, when she was trying to get out of the hallway. Which was when she said she'd been wanting to get rid of all that stuff for years."

"All the stuff in the hallway?" queried Franc. "I thought she was a hoarder."

"So did I," said Sam. "So I immediately said we could have the place cleared."

"And?"

"She seemed surprised. Like that was something that could never happen. Then I pointed out that if she was going to be on crutches, there was no way she could come and go from her flat unless the hall was empty."

Franc was nodding.

"She thought about that for a while then kind of grunted in agreement, before saying I'd have to do everything myself. "It's bad enough getting His Lordship round to shut the door" were her words."

"The son," guessed Franc. "Which door?"

"Back door."

Sam was shaking his head in amazement, as he recollected what the old woman had told him. "It locks at the top. I unbolt it with me stick, but only if His Lordship agrees to come round to lock it again at night. Too high for me, and stiff as steel. Terrible neighborhood we live in. Dreadful neighborhood! Got to keep locked up. Even then, I have to feed him."

"You mean …"

"Three times a week. And he begrudges me even that! His own mother!"

"He only comes round to lock your back door?"

"Least he could do, the sniveling toe rag!"

"What if Bronnie and I were to do it? Lock your back door in the evenings?"

"You'd do that?" she'd stared at him, disbelieving.

"What do you do on the other four days of the week?" Sam had asked. "Like, when you don't unlock it?"

"Have to keep the thing shut," she said. Although not as politely as that. "Sometimes the fumes in the place—it's unbearable!"

"Have you thought about changing the lock on the …"

"Landlord won't pay!" she rebutted, before he'd even finished. Then after a pause, "No need to look at me in that tone of voice. We're not millionaires!"

"So," Franc was trying to process all this. "The ugly rows. The smell of kippers. The hallway clutter. They could all be a thing of the past?"

"It's looking hopeful," agreed Sam.

"All because you took in those flowers."

"You know how Geshe Wangpo told us about wisdom, compassion and power? There's not a lot you can do sometimes, unless there's some kind of circuit-breaker. A shift in power, presenting an opportunity."

"And you were ready for the opportunity," observed Franc, approvingly.

"I guess."

"A lot of other people would have left the flowers to die."

"I would have left the flowers to die, if it wasn't for Geshe Wangpo. And we would never have found out what was really going on downstairs. Of course, Bronnie and I will get a new lock fitted to the old girl's kitchen door. It's a small price to pay for peaceful evenings and kipper-free mornings." Sam's eyes gleamed bright with anticipation.

Franc was nodding thoughtfully, before a roguish smile appeared on his face. "You'll also have to find a way to cope with the downside," he observed.

"Downside?"

"Sure. Looks like you're at serious risk of losing your Precious Treasure!"

That evening I sat at my open, first-floor window, gazing out across the courtyard, with the peaceful chanting of monks in the temple and the mélange of incense, catnip and frangipani blossom wafting on the breeze. As I looked out into the darkness, I felt another, uneasy sensation. Every time there was a stirring in the shadows, a movement next to the trunk of a tree, I couldn't help wondering: was it the tabby? So used to enjoying this world as my own domain, it seemed I could no longer take for granted my unfettered prowling up the road to the place I had thought of as my home away from home. I even had to look over my shoulder on my short excursions to The Himalaya Book Café.

I knew that the tabby, like Mrs. Williams, was my Precious Treasure. That for my own benefit, the best way for me to deal with his presence was to think of him just the way that Geshe Wangpo had instructed—a special case, whose every suffering I wished to remove and whose happiness I yearned for. A being designed for my cultivation of equanimity, compassion and love.

Yes, I knew all of this, but after what had happened to Sam, I couldn't help wondering if I'd ever experience a shift like he had. Or was I stuck with my own Precious Treasure forever?

CHAPTER FIVE

GROOMING. IT'S ONE OF THOSE THINGS WE ALL HAVE TO DO. But isn't it wonderful, dear reader, when someone else does it for you?

These were my precise thoughts one early summer morning, as I stood on the desk in His Holiness' Executive Assistants' office, as Tenzin performed his most important task of the day—brushing my coat. Always early into work, Tenzin would arrive looking every inch the consummate diplomat that he was; suited and booted, with an air that promised the utmost discretion, his hands bearing a faint tang of carbolic from the soap he used. As soon as he had transferred items from his briefcase to his desk, and surveyed whatever had arrived by overnight courier, his next task was to retrieve a brush with fine bristles from his top drawer and step over to where I was standing on the edge of his desk, tail held high in anticipation.

For the next few minutes, he gently swept the brush through my coat, removing great clouds of cream-colored fur. Fur that would otherwise be cast off onto the intricately-woven rugs and embroidered runners that bedecked the household. Fur that would blow like tumbleweed down the stairs and through the passageways of the Dalai Lama's residence. Fur that I molted in such profusion at this time of the year, that I only needed to brush up against the dark-suited leg of a visiting dignitary to leave a generous swatch of cream behind, as a no-doubt greatly treasured memento. Tenzin, who was punctilious about all matters diplomatic, regarded the morning comb as a way to pre-empt such feline displays.

And so we stood there, Tenzin carefully working his way up one side of my furry form and down the other. Me offering an encouraging purr. What a wonderful morning ritual! Through the open window, you could taste the freshness of the Himalayas on the early morning air. In the trees outside, barbets and babblers chattered with irrepressible joy. There was a sense of new possibilities, of a fresh day's adventures. And as if to complete the gladness, a short while later there was the unmistakable aroma of coffee. Moments later, Oliver stepped into their shared office, bearing a cardboard tray with two big flat whites. Yes, dear reader, the 'first thing in the morning coffee ritual' had reached even the rarefied heights of Dharamshala.

"Already started the most important business of the day!" observed Oliver, putting the tray down on the desk.

"Look how much has come off already, and I've only just started," Tenzin indicated a paper bag half full of my discarded coat, and held up the brush, clogged with cream fur. After thanking Oliver for the coffee and taking an appreciative sip, he continued the brushing. "I never cease to be amazed how much comes off her."

"Enough to make a whole other cat," joked Oliver.

I gave him a blue-eyed gaze. For an intelligent man, he often said such silly things. I put it down to that puzzling sense of humor people referred to as 'British'.

"Certainly enough fur for another cat." Tenzin pulled another clump off his brush and dropped it into the paper bag.

Oliver sipped his coffee contemplatively. "Yet furry as she is, HHC is not her fur."

Tenzin glanced over at him, as though acknowledging something significant in what he'd said. "Nor is she her nails," he said, bringing back an unwelcome memory of the day before, when the two of them had attended to my nails. Ever since the incident of the ingrowing nails, the two men had been extra-vigilant in the nail-trimming department.

"Nor is she her teeth," said Oliver. Several months before I'd had to visit the vet, Dr Axel Munthe, who had removed a badly decayed tooth—under anesthetic of course.

"Nor any body part," agreed Tenzin. The two men seemed to be playing some kind of game which required them to state the obvious. Of course I wasn't a body part! If every organ of my body was to be removed and set out for inspection, not a single one could be called 'the Dalai Lama's Cat'.

"But nor is she separate from her parts," said Tenzin.

"Indeed," Oliver met his eyes with a twinkle, before adding, "She is not cat food—thank heavens!"

Tenzin chuckled. "Nor Mrs. Trinci's diced chicken liver—nor any of the meals she gets down at The Himalaya Book Café."

After a while Oliver added, "She is not even buttered toast!"

They both laughed. Then Oliver said, "But she is as dependent on them as she is on her parts."

"We are what we eat," said Tenzin, pausing to sip his coffee. "And drink," he held up his mug.

Oliver nodded.

It seemed they had embarked on a curious analysis, in which they were both well versed. One which rang vague bells, but I couldn't place it for the moment. Clearly I depended on all my bodily organs, but wasn't one of them. Just as I depended on food and drink, but I wasn't them either. The statements were so self-evident, they hardly seemed worth voicing.

"And let's not forget the most subtle form of dependence," said Oliver.

Coming to the end of our session, Tenzin put down his brush and massaged the base of my ears with his fingertips, just the way I liked it. "Dependence on mind's projection?" he offered.

"Exactly."

At that moment, Mrs. Trinci appeared in the doorway, carrying a plate bearing freshly baked pastries. "*Buon giorno!* A little morsel to start the day?"

Having come in early to prepare lunch, she had evidently prepared a little something special for His Holiness and his staff, as was her wont.

Tenzin and Oliver were effusive in their thanks, but the moment Mrs. Trinci had stepped into their office and caught sight of me, she was oblivious to them. Shoving the plate in Oliver's direction, she stepped over to me. "The Most Beautiful Creature That Ever Lived!" she enthused, showering me with kisses. I was engulfed in her perfume, and the clanking of the bracelets on her arms. "How are you my little *tesorino*?!"

Looking up from where she held me in her embrace, I saw Oliver catch Tenzin's eye with a glint of amusement. "Little *tesorino*," he repeated in his English accent.

"What's wrong with that?" Mrs. Trinci drew herself up in faux defiance.

"We know her as HHC."

She shrugged as though this was of little consequence.

"At the old people's home, they know her as the Therapy Cat," said Tenzin.

"Who is right?" asked Oliver. "Which version is she?"

Understanding that a subtle point was being made, Mrs. Trinci, who had been meditating for several years replied, "Once I would have said that my version is right. Obviously!" She regarded both men from beneath her mascaraed eyelashes with irrepressible brio. "I have learnt that there are as many versions of the Dalai Lama's Cat as there are minds to perceive her ..."

"You're absolutely right Mrs. Trinci!" beamed Oliver.

"But I still like my own the best!"

They all burst out laughing.

That afternoon, I decided to return to my volunteering job at the old folks' home. Over the past six weeks, I had come to enjoy my sessions as Therapy Cat, and the better I got to know the people there, the more I enjoyed them.

Setting out along the road, I was on Full Tabby Alert. Even though the nursing home was only a short walk away, ever since my fateful outing to 21 Tara Crescent, the tabby had felt like a foreboding presence. Who was to say that he wouldn't be lurking by the very gates of Namgyal Monastery, just as he had the first time I'd encountered him? Or lounging proprietorially in a much-loved spot I believed to be my own? The side of my face had felt raw for days after our first skirmish and I knew that if things got really nasty, I would come out of the combat very badly indeed.

Which was why I was extra watchful. Checking the vicinity every step of the way. Making sure I had plenty of space around me—and the presence of people who might step in, if the worst was to happen.

I made it along the road and up the steps to the garden. Busy looking all around, it was a few moments before I looked directly ahead to the bench in the garden under the cedar tree. Unusually, it was occupied—and by someone I recognized. I paused, regarding him carefully, taking in the tousled dark hair and tanned skin of the young man from the temple and also The Himalaya Book Café. The one who Serena had described as 'quite intense'.

He glanced over, noticing me appear in the garden with neither interest nor displeasure. I saw he had a notebook and pen in his lap, but wasn't writing anything. He was gazing at something in the distance—or maybe at nothing at all.

I continued cautiously, skirting around the lawn behind him to keep out of his way. I was about to cross the flowerbed and head into the rockery, when the sound of rushing paws scrambling up the steps from the road was followed by the appearance of Marcel, then Kyi Kyi.

Franc would sometimes bring them up the road for a walk. It seemed that's exactly what had happened that afternoon. Having caught my scent, they had pursued it, bursting into the garden and hoping to play chase. They raced over in my direction, expecting me to scramble up the tree to get away from them.

But as you already know, I am not that sort of cat—and you are most certainly not the kind of reader to be interested in trite canine distractions. Instead of obeying primitive instinct, I stood my ground, staring the two of them down. Having gained considerable momentum, Marcel had to slam on the brakes, reaching forward with both front paws to avoid a head-on collision. Kyi Kyi jostled to an unsteady halt behind him, looking altogether bewildered behind his shaggy eyebrows.

I heard Franc chuckle, as he appeared in the garden. "Picked the wrong cat, boys!" he noted, as the dogs rolled on the lawn, acting like they'd only ever come across to say hello. I noticed Franc's shoelace trailing beside him as he walked.

"Sorry for the interruption," he looked over at the young man with an apologetic shrug.

"No interruption," replied the other, with a European accent. "I was just … sitting."

"Nice place to sit," agreed Franc, perching at the other end of the bench under the cool of the tree, to tie up his loose shoelace.

There was something nurturing about that towering cedar with its limbs stretching almost the full distance of the lawn, its gnarled and ancient trunk, its umbrella-like branches protecting any being beneath from sun or snow.

"I think I've seen you at the café," said Franc, after he'd finished his knot. "I'm Franc, the maître d'."

"Conrad," the young man extended his arm along the bench somewhat formally. "I like your café. A place of sanctuary and connection—East and West."

"Thank you," Franc smiled, surprised. "That's the most beautiful way I've ever heard it described. And exactly what we want to achieve."

Regarding the young man closely, he seemed to be making his mind up about something before he said, "Your question the other night at Geshe Wangpo's class was also very perceptive."

It was Conrad's turn to look surprised. "Who am I to become enlightened?" he repeated the question word for word. "You were there?" Then as Franc nodded, "It is the question I have wrestled with for years. The question that brought me from Geneva to Dharamshala."

"One way or another," Franc spoke after a pause. "It is the question each one of us has to face in our journey. In the West especially, many of us have a strong sense of unworthiness. Incapacity."

"Lama Wangpo. I found his presence disturbing for this reason."

"Really?" Franc raised his eyebrows.

"He makes me feel so ... dirty."

"It would never be his intention."

"For several years, I have wanted to meet someone like him." Conrad had a faraway look in his eyes. "An authentic guru. A yogi. Someone who has seen the truth personally and can teach me how to see it too. In Switzerland, you only read about such people. Or perhaps they may visit and give a talk from the front of a hall, but you can never get close to them. I wanted to spend time in the presence of such a teacher, to learn at his feet in the time-honored way. Perhaps to devote my life to him. That's why I decided to come to India.

"So I saved and saved. I took on a second job, and then a third when I finished university. As soon as I had enough money, I came here. Only to discover that the brightness of such beings is unbearable. And I hadn't left my old self back in Europe. He had come with me. Sitting in that gompa is too much for me. I can't get past my own darkness."

Burying his face in his hands, Conrad looked utterly dismayed. Franc regarded the serious-minded young man with concern. His comment about what Conrad had asked in class, a few evenings before, had opened the floodgates in a way he certainly hadn't anticipated. Conrad evidently needed to unburden himself. Was he perhaps traveling alone and suffering from the lack of an opportunity to express his feelings to someone who might understand?

But how to respond? Even Marcel and Kyi Kyi seemed subdued, as they snuffled around the bench. Franc looked nonplussed. He was no stranger to intense young seekers who showed up in Dharamshala. He had been one himself. It was the suddenness of Conrad's outburst and its magnitude that had shaken him.

"It's not unusual to have feelings of inadequacy," Franc commented after a long pause.

Conrad shook his face before raising his head and gazing into the middle distance. Being inadequate, it seemed, didn't even begin to describe the way he felt. Things were evidently very much worse than that. When he finally spoke, his words were contorted with grief.

Looking at Franc directly he confessed, "I killed my brother."

Franc was startled.

"On a motorbike on a pass to Innsbruck."

"When you say "killed" …?"

"There were five of us in the group. Three bikes. Two people, two people, one person. He was not so experienced, so he was the passenger of our friend, Stiegs. I know he wants to take control, so at a break in the afternoon I said, for a short time, he can take my bike. I joined Stiegs.

"We came to a sharp corner. The light was poor and there was ice on the road. He's in front and going too fast. We see it all like in slow motion—the slide, the overcorrection. The full-on collision with a truck."

Conrad shuddered. After the longest while he continued, "It is hard to get past such a thing."

Franc was nodding.

"For the rest of my life I must blame myself. The stupidity! The madness of what I decided. The never-ending guilt; he was my mother's favorite." He gulped, "I don't think I can ever shake off this heaviness." Putting his hands behind his head he folded down on himself, till his face was between his knees.

"How long ago?" asked Franc.

"Five years on the fifteenth of December."

"So, for the past five years you've been ..."

"Black with sin," Conrad glanced up at Franc inconsolably. Franc regarded him with a compassionate expression.

After a few moments when he didn't respond, Conrad spoke from his crushed posture, "Perhaps you want to tell me not to blame myself. This is what my friends say. My parents, also. If I went to see Geshe Wangpo, he would probably say this too."

Franc was shrugging.

Conrad didn't know how to take his reaction, so he asked, "You don't think so?"

"One thing I've learnt is not to predict how my guru will respond. Often, a teacher will come out with something that's the last thing you'd expect. You see when we're unhappy, without realizing it, we can get so locked into a particular way of thinking that it's hard for us to imagine there's a different way.

Wiser beings, however, see other possibilities."

Conrad was frowning. He prompted, "So, Buddhism would say I **should** blame myself?"

"I don't think so," Franc responded calmly.

"So, what would Buddhism say?" Folded down, hands on his shoes, Conrad seemed braced as if for a physical beating.

It was a long while before Franc spoke. When he did, there was a surprising firmness to his tone, one which reminded me of someone else—but I couldn't place who it was, to begin with.

"If I give you an answer, you must promise to listen through to the end, no matter how strange it may seem."

Conrad shrugged as if there was little Franc could say that would make matters worse.

"This self of yours that is black with sin, that is cloaked in darkness. Do you have any doubt who this self is?"

"None," Conrad shot back.

"You know him. You feel him. You have a strong sense of him?"

"Unfortunately, yes."

"Then I want you to help me find him."

Conrad grunted his assent.

"And remember—all the way to the end. So," he took a deep breath, "is this guilty self the little toe of your left foot?"

Conrad didn't so much shake his head as twitch it sharply sideways. "What strangeness is this?"

"You only have to answer yes or no."

"No, then. Of course not!"

"Any of the other toes in your left foot?"

"It has nothing to do with my left foot. Or my leg."

"And, I take it, not the right foot or leg either?"

"Definitely not."

"Good. Then moving up the body, is this guilty self located in some organ of your abdomen?"

Conrad glanced up to see whether Franc was making some perverse joke at his expense.

Methodically, Franc continued through every part of his torso, his hands and arms, shoulders and neck and head. And as he did so, I realized who he was being like—Geshe Wangpo himself! And unless I was very much mistaken, this was an analysis which Geshe-la used to lead during meditations in the temple, the one that had been ringing distant bells earlier, when Tenzin had been brushing my coat. Franc, Geshe Wangpo's student for many years now, had become so familiar with it, that not only could he repeat the exercise, he seemed to embody the manner of his teacher—the mind of the guru somehow merging with that of the student.

I realized that it was exactly this exercise Tenzin and Oliver had been referring to this morning, during my grooming session. HHC was not my fur, my nails, my teeth. Whether the self one was trying to find was that of an intense young Swiss man, or the fluffiest of Himalayan cats, it involved an identical process.

It is the same for each one of us, whoever we are. And even you, dear reader. The self that can be the cause of such pain or heartache, the self that grieves the loss of love or hope, the self that is fearful or anxious—where exactly is this troublesome self located?

"What about your brain?" Franc asked, once they'd arrived at the uppermost part of his body.

"Now there … perhaps," said Conrad.

"Your brain is your guilty self?" checked Franc. Then, responding to Conrad's ambivalence, "If an exact replica of your brain was to be placed in front of you, along with the replica brains of ten other people, would you be able identify your self, as easily as you could in a photograph of ten people?"

Conrad shrugged. "I guess not. But where else could the self be?"

"Perhaps we are looking in the wrong place," Franc suggested. "What if the self is not a physical entity at all. What if it is an aspect of consciousness?"

"Makes sense," said Conrad, hitching himself up so that he was now resting his elbows on his knees.

"So … eye consciousness. Is that your guilty self?"

Conrad shook his head.

"Sound consciousness? Scent consciousness?" Franc went through each of the five senses systematically, receiving Conrad's denial, before he arrived at a final type of consciousness. "There is only one kind of consciousness left," he said. "Mental consciousness. That's the only place we haven't explored."

Conrad looked up, "That must be it. That's where the self must be."

Franc regarded him carefully. "Very well. Mental consciousness comprises different parts. Remember, we are trying to find the guilty self. The one you told me a moment ago that you feel very strongly. The one you can't possibly escape. Is this self to be found in your negative thoughts or your positive thoughts?"

"That," said Conrad, "is an interesting philosophical question."

"I'm not talking philosophy," countered Franc. You said earlier you had no problem identifying your self that is black with sin …"

"Of course!"

"So, negative thoughts or positive ones?"

Conrad shrugged, "I suppose negative ones?"

"Okay," Franc nodded. "Consciousness is a continuity of mind moments. A stream of thoughts, sensations and experiences, one after another, constantly throughout the day. Which particular negative thought is your guilty self?"

"Many of them."

"You have many selves?"

"Of course not. Just one."

I could tell that Conrad was now zeroing in on this exercise with particular intensity.

Franc continued, "When you said your self is to be found in negative thoughts, which particular negative thought is the self you feel yourself so strongly to be?"

Conrad looked perplexed. "How can this be? When I look for it, it is not to be found." Slowly, a wry expression was creeping across his face, as if the truth behind this most curious analysis was beginning to dawn.

Franc allowed what he had just said to sink in a bit before confirming, "Your self cannot be found in any part of your physical body?"

"No, no."

"And even in your mind, your consciousness …"

"When I look, it is … unfindable!" His face lit up with astonishment.

"Very good!" Franc smiled, encouragingly. "But you still have a strong sense of self?"

"Of course."

"So what is this self, if it isn't a permanent physical or mental phenomenon?"

Conrad raised himself to a normal seated position as he considered this. And the faintest hint of a smile began to creep across his face as he said, "Perhaps it is a concept. Only an idea."

Franc raised his eyebrows in droll confirmation. "Apart from concept," he confirmed, "there is no self. It is just an idea. A notion. A thing that comes and goes. A story we tell ourselves about our experience of reality that's changing the whole time, sometimes up, sometimes down. Depending on who we've just been speaking to, and what we've been eating and drinking, our ideas and feelings about our self change, which just goes to show that there's nothing permanent there. It's just a thought."

The smile on Conrad's face was growing bigger and bigger.

"To come up with such a concept," continued Franc, "then to tell ourselves that this self we have concocted is a permanent thing, and is guilty, sinful, cloaked in darkness—why create such a negative fantasy?"

"So the self don't exist at all?" asked Conrad.

"That's going too far," Franc raised a finger. "That idea is called "nihilism" and is a great mistake."

"But when I looked, I couldn't find it."

"What you need to understand is that there is a true "I" and a false "I". The true "I" is the label you apply to all this," he wiggled his index finger while scanning down Conrad's body. "It is your body, your history, your likes and dislikes, the collection of things that go to make up the idea of Conrad. What Buddhists call "the conventionally-accepted I".

"The other is the false "I". It is the idea that there is an independent self that exists somehow separately from body and mind, some inherently existing being that has qualities such as being guilty or successful or depressed or popular. Such a being doesn't exist. It can't exist. It never has existed. It's just a tale we are making up."

"So why do we feel it so strongly?" asked Conrad.

"Habit," said Franc. "From the youngest age, we learn to identify with this invisible self. We have ideas about it. We try to project it out into the world in a particular way. But other people don't have the same ideas about our self that we do. If I called ten people who know you, I would get ten slightly different accounts of Conrad. One might tell me about Conrad who, being a kind and caring brother, gave his younger sibling a chance to ride his motorbike, because he knew how eager he was to have a turn. I would hear stories different from Conrad's own account. And even Conrad's own account would vary, depending on what kind of mood he was in," Franc smiled playfully. "Perhaps after he has had a few steins of beer, he isn't quite such an unhappy fellow?"

"It's true," shrugged Conrad.

I was reminded about how, only that morning, Tenzin and Oliver had had a similar discussion with Mrs Trinci about me. How she had told them, to their great amusement, that she had learnt that there are as many versions of the Dalai Lama's Cat as there are minds to perceive her—but she still liked her own version the best!

"All of which goes to show," said Franc, "that this "self" is just an idea. A concept."

"So when we die," asked Conrad earnestly, "there is nothing?"

Franc held his gaze. "Remember what we set out to find?"

"The guilty self."

"Which was not there. But at no point did we doubt the existence of consciousness. It is only because we are conscious that we are able to carry out such a search. Subtle consciousness continues through all our experiences, like string through the beads of a necklace. It is probably Buddha's greatest discovery that he recognized that consciousness doesn't need to involve a self, and that this self is just an idea. Like Copernicus, who came after him and discovered that the sun doesn't travel round the earth but the other way around, in one way Buddha's discovery changes everything, but in another it changes nothing. The sun still seems to rise in the east and set in the west, but we know that is just an illusion. In the same way, we seem to have an independent self, but that, too, is just an illusion. For many of us," his eyes narrowed as he met Conrad's expression, "an unnecessary burden. As the great Shantideva says:

If all the injury,
Fear and pain in this world
Arise from grasping at a self,
Then what use is that great ghost to me?"

Sitting fully upright now, and gazing into the garden with a quiet smile, Conrad murmured, "You have given me much food for thought."

"Good," said Franc.

"I can blame myself but, as you imply, where is the self that I am blaming?"

"You've got it!"

"Is there a name for it, this method, this analysis you've just described?"

"It goes by a variety of names. It is sometimes called "suchness", the way that things exist. Or "dependent origination", because every thing exists in dependence on factors other than itself. Or the most simple term, the Sanskrit word *sunyata.*"

Sunyata was a word the Dalai Lama often used. And it had been one of the four main concepts he'd said should be included in a book describing Tibetan Buddhism, along with turning away from suffering, and cultivating the ultimate form of loving kindness—bodhicitta.

"As concepts go, sunyata is a bit of slippery fish," said Franc. "You think you've got it and then, whoosh! You don't. You end up with a something, or with a nothing. But always remember, the question is not about whether things exist or not, but **how** they exist."

"How they exist," intoned Conrad, committing this to memory.

"And while understanding the concept is useful, the real benefit is meditating on it. Experiencing the meaning of sunyata in a state of mental clarity."

"I can imagine," said Conrad, enthusiasm coming into his voice for the first time. "This is why the lamas are so bright! Teachers like Geshe Wangpo—they experience these things directly."

"Probably," smiled Franc.

"Their radiance! The feeling that they have no boundaries! For them, the experience of consciousness must be so different."

Franc was nodding. "Unlike most of us, I don't think they experience themselves as this bag of bones. As this tiny, little limited me, myself and I."

For a while, Conrad met his gaze before he said with feeling, "I am so glad that you stopped here on your walk today."

"It's always a pleasure to share the Dharma," Franc replied, rising to his feet, seeming like Geshe Wangpo even in his manner of doing that.

"You have helped me so much …" Conrad brought a hand to his heart, "here. In a way I would never have expected."

Franc smiled broadly, taking a step back and slapping his leg to get the dogs' attention.

"Dharma means Buddha's teachings—yes?" checked Conrad.

Franc nodded, "It also means the end of suffering."

Not long after Franc and the dogs departed, Conrad left the garden too. He made his way down the steps with a lightness I hadn't seen in him before.

For my own part, dear reader, I was touched by the same sense of release as well. And in my own way, with a profound sense of peace. What a burden it can sometimes be, to be HHC, Rinpoche, Swami, and The Most Beautiful Creature That Ever Lived! What a delight to find that those terms, like so many leaves caught up in a summer breeze, lack substance or any real importance—they are ideas that aren't even necessary.

Making my way up the rockery and pushing through the dark green leaves and stems of the agapanthus, it occurred to me that here, in this place, was all the proof I needed of how liberating the truth could be. At the retirement home, I hadn't been known by any of my names or titles. No-one had brought their palms together at the heart because I was the Dalai Lama's Cat. They weren't responding to me because of some perceived identity or association. I had simply appeared and practiced loving kindness. And those visits had been among the happiest moments of my life.

Today, my visit followed the same pattern as in previous weeks—at least, to begin with. Rita and Neville, who I had come to learn would sit out on the veranda whenever they had the chance, heralded my arrival with excited cries of "She's here!" and "Therapy Cat!"

After smooching them and few others on the canvas chairs outside, I made my way through the open doors to where the room of sedentary seniors began to stir. The woman in the wheelchair, Yvette, demanded my attention loudly. On the sofa, Christopher, the artist and 'cheeky devil', was among the more active wanting me to join him.

Hilda, in the alcove, was always one of the first I'd go to, but today I arrived to find her armchair empty. For a moment I paused, staring up at the empty space she usually occupied.

"She's not with us this morning, my dear. She's in her room, resting," explained Yvette.

After a moment I made my way around the lounge, making sure to recollect bodhicitta motivation, while rubbing against the limbs or purring appreciatively for the benefit of the residents. Each one of them responded in their own way, some seeking comfort from touching another flesh-and-blood being, others wanting the acknowledgement of a purr or a gentle headbutt.

Instead of leaving through the veranda door as usual, I headed in the opposite direction, along a wide corridor through which residents came and went from their rooms. I had never ventured this far inside before and was heading deep into unknown territory—always a dangerous undertaking for a cat with unsteady gait. Guided by instinct, I continued around a corner and along a lengthier passage, passing by a number of closed doors until I came to one which was ajar. Detecting a movement inside, I peeked through a gap above the door hinge; Hilda was lying on a hospital-style bed, hooked up to her breathing tubes. Leaning over her was a middle-aged woman.

At a glance I surmised that they were mother and daughter. Hilda's visitor was trying her best to maintain a calm demeanor while attending to her frail, limp mother, a diminished form in the midst of all those tubes and machinery.

The bed was next to windows overlooking a garden, bright in the Himalayan morning. Several of the windows were open and through them came the drone of a distant lawnmower, the tang of freshly cut grass, the flurry of magpies in the trees. The ceiling shimmered silver with the reflected surface of a water fountain outside.

For all the activity going on in the world just beyond this room, however, there could be no doubting what was going on inside it. I may have been here only moments, but it was enough to recognize that Hilda wasn't simply resting. We cats are highly intuitive in certain ways, dear reader. I had no sense of an imminent departure, but I was in no doubt that Hilda was, gently and slowly, leaving this existence behind.

As I appeared around the side of the door, the woman next to Hilda looked up with surprise.

"Oh, Mum!" she gestured. "It's true—she's just the same as Bella!"

As I stepped into the room, Hilda rolled her head over on the pillow. She was even paler than before. As I made my way closer, the daughter observed, "Looks like she's come to see you!"

The bed was much too high for me to reach unaided, but Hilda's daughter knew exactly what to do. Lifting me, she placed me carefully near the foot of the bed. Hilda was too weak to move very much, but I knew she was watching me closely. Slowly—and only after first testing the blanket with my paw—I began my way up the bed, on the side opposite the daughter. Hilda's right arm was lying outside the bedclothes, and I made my way between it and the narrow hump of her body, until I was as close as I could get without sitting on her chest.

"Oh!" Hilda's daughter whispered beside us. "How special is this?"

Once settled, I looked directly into Hilda's eyes. It is a rare privilege for a cat to allow full, eye-to-eye contact with a human, but I held her gaze with my large, aquamarine eyes, trying—like the Dalai Lama himself—to communicate something of the boundless light and love that was the true nature of Hilda's mind, whatever the constraints and diminution of her physical form.

Despite her pallor, her eyes were alert. Vitality may have been ebbing from her body, but for this moment at least, her consciousness was undimmed. She was eager to engage.

I looked at Hilda, sensing how frail her physical form had become, but how strong her attention was. Franc's words about teachers and yogis were suddenly very appropriate: *Unlike most of us, I don't think they experience themselves as this bag of bones. As this tiny, little limited 'me, myself and I'.*

For my own part, I knew this to be true. I sat in meditation with the Dalai Lama every day and the feeling was oceanic. His benevolence without limit. There was never any sense that his consciousness was somehow restricted to a robed, physical form, or some narrow sense of personal identity. It was exactly

because he had let go of any such identification that his was such a powerful presence.

I wanted to convey as much of this feeling to Hilda as I could, so I did so in the best way I knew how: I began to purr.

A smile formed about her lips. I felt a slight squeeze of pressure from where her arm ran down the side of my body. More than anything, she seemed to respond to what I was trying to convey by the way she was looking at me; her eyes may have been old and have few things left in this world to see, but they reflected back such profound peace I felt that she was somehow resonating with an energetic presence that had nothing to do with name or form.

As I purred and she smiled, I thought how wonderful was this *sunyata* of which the wise ones spoke, especially near the time of death. Because if it could be truly understood and felt, if one fully realized there was no inherently existing self—no 'me, myself and I' with all its passions and melodramas, fables and fantasies—then who exactly was dying? What was being lost? Did it not make intuitive sense, deep within our heart, that all that was happening was the most subtle form of consciousness slipping out from the heart of this particular experience of reality to whatever awaited next?

For the longest time Hilda smiled, and I purred. And on that bright, Himalaya morning, the room was filled with peace and light. A state that went much deeper than the mere acceptance of what was happening, even approaching a sense of joyful anticipation at what was to come. A transition from pain, enfeeblement and restriction to boundless radiance and bliss.

When Hilda's daughter made a sound, I looked up to see a tear rolling down her cheek. A tear not of sadness, but of love. And I knew she could feel it too.

It was early afternoon when I made my way home to Namgyal Monastery. I left both Hilda and her daughter enjoying a siesta, and returned down the familiar roadside. As I did, I looked out for the tabby. Though perhaps with less vigilance than on my way out this morning. Franc's explanation of sunyata to Conrad, and my later experience with Hilda, made me feel curiously uplifted.

It is said that you need to hear the concept of dependent arising explained for thousands of hours before you truly understand its profound personal consequences. I had heard many teachings from Geshe Wangpo. And had felt it embodied in the presence of His Holiness every day of my life. Was I, perhaps, a cat who was leaving behind mundane reality with all its irritations? If I no longer identified with a self-absorbed and somewhat pampered Himalayan, would that not mean I could deal with any future tabby encounter with cool sublimity? Had I gone beyond 'me, myself and I' and all the defensive posturing that went with it? Had I thrown aside my ego as an irrelevance, a burden that afflicted only less-enlightened felines?

As it happened, there was no tabby to be seen on the road home. Nor at the Namgyal gates. What I was able to detect, as I arrived home, was the delightful aroma of Mrs. Trinci's cooking.

I remembered how she had arrived at work early that morning because she'd had a VIP meal to prepare. Lunch would be over, at least for the guests, but even when I wasn't present for such occasions, I was never forgotten. Mrs. Trinci would always carefully save a portion of the tastiest morsels for my delectation. These she would leave in a ramekin on a tray in a corner of the larder next to the kitchen.

I hopped onto the ground-floor ledge and through the window left open, just for me. As I made my way along the short corridor, I began to salivate. Unless I was very much mistaken, Mrs Trinci had prepared one of my favorite casseroles, involving the most succulent morsels and richest of gravies. Waves of the tantalizing fragrance rolled towards me, as if it was being deliberately stirred to arouse my interest. Whiskers quivering, I hastened towards it.

Rounding the kitchen corner, I spotted the ramekin Mrs. Trinci had put out for me. But my attention was instantly fixed on something very different. Something so horrifying I could scarcely believe it. A malevolent, hunched presence, rapidly devouring my own special treat. The tabby!

CHAPTER SIX

I FELT AN INSTANT SURGE OF ADRENALIN. THE INSTINCT NOT for flight—but fight! The interloper was in **my** house. Eating **my** food. How dare he!

From across the room, I yowled in anger. Instinctively he leapt, spinning in mid-air to face me. As he did, his rear paw struck the ramekin, sending it skating against a door frame with a chime of porcelain.

I puffed up in size, fur on end. Heading directly towards him I paused, staring into those hideous yellow eyes. I delivered one final, low, baleful warning.

His gaze was locked on me. But I could tell he was considering his options. The corridor behind me, leading to the open window. The kitchen door to the side, opening to a loading zone.

I wasn't waiting. Impelled to attack, to protect my domain, whatever the consequence, I leapt onto him, lashing my front paws wildly. Taken aback, he threw me off, shrugging away before launching a counterstrike with his front right paw.

It seemed like the whole world was shrieking with fury, as I lunged at him again. This time he spun round, kicking viciously with both back legs. Rear claws fully extended, the brute force of the thrust knocked me off balance. I skidded across the floor, just like the ramekin.

He was about to pounce onto me, straight for the jugular, when I realized the screaming was coming from the VIP chef! Mrs. Trinci was looming over us, wooden spoon in hand. The tabby had a choice: sink his fangs into me—or make his escape.

He chose the latter, springing from a crouched position towards the open kitchen door. In the same moment I was back on my feet. I had to pursue him. I wasn't going to let him get away with it. The dynamics had changed dramatically in my favor. It was time to wreak revenge!

Suddenly, I felt the restraining hand of Mrs. Trinci followed by a crash from outside, as the gate into the kitchen courtyard slammed shut. There was an interminable period of shouting between Mrs. Trinci and a security guard. What on earth was going on? Heart pounding and unable to think, there was no way I could move. Mrs. Trinci held me down firmly.

In the next moment, another guard appeared—one of the men who controlled access to the Dalai Lama's private residence. Scooping me up, he held me in an iron grip as he took me upstairs and along the corridor. Not into His Holiness' apartment, which was currently closed; not even to the Executive Assistants' office. He quickly slid me into the First Aid Room, before closing the door shut.

I was reduced to dead silence. Charged with adrenalin, I paced about the room. It was a small area, rarely used, with white walls and sills too high to jump onto. The most overwhelming sensation was the antiseptic odor coming from the hand sanitizer on the wall by the washbasin. I walked round and round. Distracted, on edge.

From outside came the sounds of security men to-ing and fro-ing, hurrying up and down the stairs. It sounded like they were involving the Executive Assistants—I heard the muffled voices of Tenzin and Oliver. Where were they going? What had happened to the intruder? Had he escaped or had they trapped him in the kitchen courtyard? If they caught him, what would happen next? Would he be returned to 21 Tara Crescent?

As the rumpus continued, I couldn't help but recollect that first encounter when he'd ambushed me near the gates. That had been bad enough, shaking me out of the feline-free complacency in which I'd lived for so long. Much worse had been discovering that he'd usurped my place at 21 Tara Crescent. He was not some random alley tom, but now a permanent fixture in the lives of Serena, Sid and Zahra, whose home and hearts were now off limits, it seemed.

To return to my own inner sanctum and discover him invading that as well—where was it all going to end? And what was I to do? Did this mean I couldn't even go downstairs without fear of being attacked?

I didn't know what to make of any of it.

As abruptly as all the activity outside had started, it came to a halt. The stark, clinical quietude of the First Aid Room began to feel all-pervasive. It was a room I knew well. In my early days at Namgyal, I used to go there with Tenzin and sit on the bed beside him, as he ate his lunch and listened to the news on BBC World Service. It had been one of those rituals, much-loved at the time, which had dwindled for no particular reason. From time to time I would still observe him step in there and would sometimes join him, for old time's sake. Always, there was a feeling of calm civility.

I began to groom myself in the middle of the carpet, cleaning off traces of saliva and fur left on my coat by the intruder.

Suddenly, the door burst open and I was picked up and showered with kisses. "Rinpoche, my poor little thing!"

It was Zahra! Followed closely by Serena and Mrs. Trinci.

"Has that tabby been stealing your food?" Sitting on the bed, she plonked me on her lap. "He's been coming to our place as well, begging for food at the kitchen door."

I looked up at her.

"Daddy found out and was very worried."

"He was," chimed in Serena. "He knew if the tabby started to hang around, you'd never be free to come."

"So he told the gardener to chase him off," continued Zahra.

I had the feeling that this was a story they were telling as much for their own, collective benefit as for mine.

"But that gardener never listens!" Mrs. Trinci clanged emphatically. "Chases every cat he sees!"

"Is that why you haven't come to see me?" Zahra seemed close to tears. Bending her head to kiss me, her dark hair fell around us both so it felt like we were in a tent, just the two of us.

"Oh, I hope he didn't throw clods of earth at you too, my little Rinpoche?"

To say I was relieved by these revelations would, dear reader, be a spectacular understatement. And there was more to come.

"We heard about a cat fight near the gates." It was Tenzin's voice. As Zahra raised her head, I saw that he had stepped into the room, Oliver behind him. They were all crammed inside the tiny room with me as the center of attention.

"More an ambush than a fight, I think," said Oliver.

"I stand corrected," agreed Tenzin. "Mr. Patel brought it to an end when he threw a pot of water over them."

Zahra was smooching me again. "Poor little thing, being bullied wherever you go."

"Well, hopefully the ordeal is over," said Serena.

"For both of them," said Tenzin, ever the diplomat. "Let's not forget, life hasn't been easy for the tabby either. To be a stray cat in Dharamshala …"

"Yes, we're very grateful to you, Oliver, for adopting him," said Serena.

"I was brought up with tabbies. Such affectionate little things."

Oliver? The tabby? Was I hearing right?

Oliver chuckled, "Don't worry, HHC. I live some distance away, so he won't trouble you again."

As Zahra scratched me with her fingernails under the chin, just the way I like it, I purred appreciatively. I'd never felt such huge relief in all my life.

"Tenzin, with His Holiness overseeing exams tonight, may we please borrow Rinpoche, just for the evening? I'd like to take her home and make things up to her."

Tenzin looked to where I was settled comfortably on her lap. "Oh, I'm sure she would be very bored sitting on her own and would much rather join you."

"We'll bring her home afterwards. We're having Yogi Tarchin for dinner and he never stays late."

"The presence of a yogi as well as culinary delights," Tenzin tilted his head with a smile. "This cat leads a more interesting life than I do!"

We left the room soon afterwards, Tenzin and Oliver back to their office, I in Zahra's arms, following Serena and Mrs. Trinci downstairs. Crossing the kitchen, we paused at the door leading to the outside courtyard. In the shadows, in what looked like a parrot cage repurposed for a rather different confinement, was the tabby. He seemed to have shrunk in size. Even though the cage was small, he looked somehow diminished. Cowering in the corner, fur flecked. As we went past he looked up, eyes fearful, limbs quaking. He was the picture of abject defeat.

"You'll be alright, Mr. Puss," Serena told him as we passed.

"More than alright," declared Mrs. Trinci. "Oliver will spoil him rotten!"

"Unlike our little darling," Serena turned to stroke my head. "Who is seldom pampered."

"Nothing ..." Mrs. Trinci didn't skip a beat as she led the way to her car, "is too good for The Most Beautiful Creature That Ever Lived!"

Which was how, dear reader, I got to spend that evening in the company of Zahra, reacquainting myself with the wonders of 21 Tara Crescent, an experience which was all the more delightful because I had thought it was lost to me forever.

As Zahra went away to boarding school, I was used to not being there for months at a time. She would return, always a little different from before. At the age of seventeen, she was now much more a young woman than a child. But the changes made no difference at all to the joy we found in each other's company. Whatever she chose to do, I was just happy to be with her.

Today she led the way across the veranda through open French doors into a large salon with cream walls and velvet sofas, and the most expansive, intricately embroidered Indian rug that felt delightful beneath the paw. We went down a corridor, past an Aladdin's cave of furnished rooms, twisting halls and flights of stairs.

In an inner courtyard, a small fountain sparkled into a fern-fringed pool where large, golden koi fish made their silent away among water lilies. Zahra and I watched them for ages, the fish so tame that when Zahra put her hand under the surface, she was able to stroke them.

Then she took me to her bedroom, a pink-walled boudoir with a white, four-poster bed, cushions everywhere, a dressing table cluttered with cosmetics, brushes and grooming paraphernalia, and fairy lights twinkling on the ceiling. All this was utterly bewitching to a cat whose only experience of bedrooms was what I knew from Namgyal Monastery.

Soon enough we were told that Yogi Tarchin had arrived and it was time to go to the dining room, which was bedecked with flowers and lit with candles especially for the occasion. The privilege of having a being like Rinpoche come to dine in one's home was bestowed on a rare few. Sid and Serena had done all they could to make it special.

There was a delightful energy in the dining room that night which rippled through all of us. Dressed in a white sherwani jacket with a Nehru collar, Sid looked every inch the Maharajah, while across the table from him in a coral-red dress and rose gold earrings, Serena glowed as his Maharani. At the head of the table as the honored guest, Rinpoche transcended his modest attire—an ochre-color shirt and brown trousers—with a lightness of spirit and a hint of humor in his warm, brown eyes that was never far below the surface.

He seemed completely unsurprised when I followed Zahra into the room, acknowledging me as a family member. Zahra sat on a chair next to Serena. While I may not have had a seat at the dining table, I hopped onto an ornate chaise nearby, where I felt just as much a part of the gathering. Champagne was served and I observed Yogi Tarchin closely as he lifted his flute in his right hand, dipping the ring finger of his left just beneath the surface of the liquid, before flicking droplets into the four directions, east, north, west and south, as an offering to all Buddhas and bodhisattvas, and for the benefit of all beings throughout universal space. In such a way, I observed, bodhicitta could be brought even to the act of drinking champagne!

Conversation flowed effortlessly around the table. This may have been their first dinner in three years, since Rinpoche had come out of his retreat, but it felt as though they had been in touch all along. In answer to Yogi Tarchin's question about their working lives, Sid described some of his own trading operations, before turning to their community activities, for which he had evident enthusiasm. These included giving children, who'd missed out on formal education, training in computer skills to help them find jobs.

Serena embroidered on what he said. Then she admitted to the greatest embarrassment of her life—the time the Dalai Lama had gone to visit her in the kitchen.

"You slammed the door on His Holiness?" Yogi Tarchin was incredulous.

"Very loudly," Serena confessed.

Yogi Tarchin began to laugh silently but heartily, his eyes crinkled shut, head thrown back and whole body shaking. It was impossible not to be caught up in his amusement.

Once he'd recovered his composure, Serena explained how she'd gone to apologize, and how the Dalai Lama had talked to her about attachment. How it applied as much to outcomes—like business success, or even falling pregnant—as to material objects and successes. How turning away from seeking happiness outside ourselves was the real start of one's spiritual journey—also known as renunciation.

"I understand the theory," Serena told Yogi Tarchin now. "I get the concept of not allowing yourself to be caught up in thoughts that make you miserable. But it's so hard! Once you're in the **habit** of focusing on certain things, how do you just shut them off?

At the head of the table, Rinpoche was nodding.

"Just like I get the concept of bodhicitta—recollecting our highest motivation throughout the day and night. But it's remembering to do it that's the hard part. Creating the mental bandwidth. How do we get rid of all the negative thoughts, to make room for positive ones?"

Yogi Tarchin allowed Serena's questions to remain as though suspended in space for a while, before dabbing his lips with his napkin and looking at her closely. "This is why meditation is at the heart of our practice," he said. "Think of meditation as mind training. Similar to physical training. When you train the body you are doing so not only for the duration of the session, but for the time between sessions. Which is most of your life. No matter where you are, or what you're doing, as a physically fit and capable person, you are better able to deal with whatever life throws at you.

"Training the mind is the same. No matter where you are or what you're doing, as a mentally fit and capable person, you are better able to deal with whatever life throws at you. All the ups and downs. You are better able to identify negative thoughts and let go of them. Just as you can find the mental space to recollect bodhicitta."

Serena glanced down at her plate with a smile. "Whenever you explain things, Rinpoche, you make them seem so obvious. So simple."

"Simple, but not easy," said Sid, exchanging a smile with Yogi Tarchin.

"And is there a particular kind of meditation that helps us manage thoughts? Create space?" asked Serena.

Yogi Tarchin nodded. "I think you may find "mind watching mind" very useful. For this, you first settle the mind to some extent, by focusing on the breath, then you pay attention to mind itself. Thoughts will naturally arise from the mind, like waves emerging from the ocean. And that's okay. Just don't engage with a thought. Get into the practice of "Acknowledge. Accept. Let go." Acknowledge each thought as a thought—don't pretend it isn't happening. Accept that you've had the thought, no matter what the nature of the thought, good or bad. And then let it go, as if you were letting go the string of a helium balloon. Allow it to simply disappear."

All three of the humans were following him closely. Me too.

"Learn to become observers."

"Observers," Serena echoed.

"It is okay to have thoughts. We all have thoughts. What's important ..." he lowered his voice, so that we all leaned closer, "is to become master of our thoughts, rather than their victim. To decide which thoughts we wish to engage with, instead of habitually engaging with every one of them—even those which cause us to be miserable.

"Imagine training in this practice to the extent that it becomes habitual. So that it is **you** who now decides what is going in your mind—not only when you meditate, but between sessions. That it is **you** who manages your thoughts, and therefore also the feelings that arise from those thoughts."

I remembered Conrad, bent forward miserably on the bench under the cedar tree, the victim of deeply negative reflection for the past five years. Serena slamming the door, as she stormed from the kitchen. Me, stalking in circles round the First Aid Room, so overwhelmed by agitation I couldn't even bear to sit down.

How amazing it would be to be able to let go of distressing thoughts instead of being overwhelmed by them!

As Serena, Sid and Zahra sat looking at Rinpoche, spellbound, he continued, "You make a wonderful discovery when you do this mind training. As you learn to consciously let go of negative thoughts, you find that they cannot exist without your attention. That they need your energy to exist at all, to keep coming back. Without your attention, they cannot remain. After a while, they stop coming back altogether, because there is no basis for their existence."

Serena was shaking her head. "How much insomnia, how much depression and anxiety are caused by too much thinking. Wouldn't it be wonderful if everyone had this knowledge, these methods!"

A dozen flames flickered about the room and the curtains rustled, as a warm breeze carried night jasmine into the room. And in that fragrant, candlelit chamber, with Yogi Tarchin explaining the subtle workings of consciousness based on a lifetime of personal observation, much of it in retreat, Sid had a question. "Of all the thoughts we have, Rinpoche, which are the most persistent? The most difficult to let go of?"

"Thoughts of self," replied Yogi Tarchin immediately, turning to him. "Of all the concepts we have, the idea of an independent "me", an "I" that exists as more than a mere label, is the most deeply-ingrained, the most instinctive impulse that we have."

Sid was nodding. "This is perhaps no surprise. We spend so much of our energy reinforcing the idea of this self. Even if we go through different stages of life and change so much, all the time we're still trying to reinforce, to concretize this feeling of 'me'."

For the first time in the conversation Zahra spoke with penetrating clarity, "Were you a different person before Mummy died?" she asked.

Shanti, Sid's first wife and Zahra's mother, was rarely mentioned. The fact that her name had come up in this particular conversation, and as Zahra's only contribution to what they were discussing, felt like a powerful invocation.

Zahra continued her questioning: "Was I a different person?"

Sid turned to look at Zahra, his eyes clouded with emotion. "I **was** a different person," he agreed. "But you were only two. I'm surprised you remember."

"I don't," she shook her head. "Nothing in particular. It was just like the sun went out. And you were so serious and sad."

Beside her, Serena reached out her arm in embrace.

"I'm alright now," she smiled after they had hugged, breaking away from Serena and looking at her father. "Everything's different. But," she paused, looking at Yogi Tarchin intently, "sometimes I wonder what happened to Mummy's consciousness. It did continue, right?"

"Of course," he nodded.

"Propelled by karma," she continued. "Her likes and dislikes. Her loves."

"Your understanding is very clear." At the other end of the table, Yogi Tarchin's eyes twinkled.

"So, if she loved Daddy and me, and was attracted back to us, does that mean any of the girls I'm friends with at school, who are a couple of years younger than I am, friends who sometimes come to visit here, could they, well, have Mummy's consciousness?"

"Zahra," Sid turned to his daughter with a smile on his face, but firmness in his tone. "We don't want our honored guest to feel like a fairground fortune teller."

"Rinpoche won't mind!" she protested, as Yogi Tarchin chuckled.

"It's alright. Okay," he held up his hands, glancing at Sid and Serena. "Better that she has questions and an interest in such things." He then fixed Zahra with a clear gaze. "Technically, you are right. She could be any of your friends. But you know, precious human rebirth, especially in a family of wealth and privilege, is not always possible."

Following him intently she raised her shoulders, "So, how would I know?"

"Unless you are clairvoyant—very difficult. But even the ordinary person, the ordinary being, can have feelings of attraction. Heart to heart."

Rocking forward in his chair there was a seriousness in his expression, "Pay attention to such feelings. We are connected to each other through innumerable lifetimes and in limitless ways. Each one of us is surrounded by mothers from many lifetimes. The tragedy is that we see most of them as complete strangers."

After dinner, we made our way to the room in 21 Tara Crescent which I was most hoping to revisit—the one at the top of the tower. Amid much laughter and joking about having eaten too much to fit up the narrow, circular stairs, the three adults ascended. Zahra, picking me up, made her way lightly after them.

It was a perfect summer night in the tower room, all four walls of which were large picture windows. I remembered the first time we had entered this place as a family, after Sid had bought the house and renovations had finally been completed. How just the four of us—Sid, Serena, Zahra and I—had stood watching the sunset, which had seemed like a celestial display put on especially for our benefit.

Tonight, in the presence of Rinpoche, it felt as though we were being blessed by the moon, blazing and imperial in the night sky, its silver beams so powerful that the icy caps of the

Himalayas glistened like an infinity of white breakers stretching as far as the eye could see.

The next window round overlooked a pine forest, its dark canopy swelling and rolling in the wind like a midnight ocean.

The third window faced onto flower beds and terraced lawns, the driveway that curved behind more trees leading to Tara Crescent. Lush and multi-colored by day, the garden was now cast in surreal monochrome. The moon and a sweeping mist of stars had transformed it into a place of intrigue, the brook that ran along the back of it whispering and burbling its secrets deep into the nearby forest.

From the fourth window Dharamshala spread out, a festival of light. McLeod Ganj above, the rest of the town below, aglow with activity and movement, though at sufficient distance to seem more like a twinkling playground than anything real.

From the tower it felt like you were up in the heavens, looking down upon a creation that was expansive and numinous. Turning to face his hosts, Yogi Tarchin's eyes reflected the wonder. "You see!" he gestured to the panoramic vistas on all four sides of us, "You already know the sensation of being objective observers."

"We are, indeed, very privileged," Sid bowed his head in agreement.

"I do find this place very peaceful," said Serena, gesturing towards the facing sofas. We all sat, Sid and Serena on one sofa, Zahra sitting next to Rinpoche, facing the mountains, on the other. I took my place on Zahra's lap.

"Are you saying," Serena wanted to confirm, "we should treat our thoughts the same way as we'd watch a passing cloud from here?"

Yogi Tarchin was nodding.

"That's how we become better at managing our thoughts?" she asked.

Rinpoche met her eyes across the room, his own flecked with silver in the moonlight. "Remember that I told you the name of this practice is "mind watching mind"? Thoughts arise from mind, and are of the same nature as mind, but there is very much more to mind than mere cognition.

"The most wonderful thing about this meditation is that it allows us to experience the nature of our own mind directly for ourselves. There is no other way to do this. All the theories people have about mind—psychologists, philosophers, neuro-scientists—all the notions they discuss and debate, these are just intellectual models. Constructs. What is better—to have a scientific model of chocolate, or to eat chocolate?" He glanced over to Zahra with a smile, his question being rhetorical, requiring no answer.

"When we practice "mind watching mind" in the gap between thoughts, even if that gap is very short, we get a direct glimpse of our own mind. And we find that it has certain qualities. We discover it is perfectly clear. Lucid. It enables anything to arise or appear—any thought, sensation, memory, whatever.

"Mind is also boundless, without beginning or end. Free from the constraints of time and space. No matter what is going on with our body, mind cannot be contained.

"Most importantly," Rinpoche was nodding, "mind has a certain feeling tone. It is not dry and cerebral, devoid of sensation. The true nature of your mind, of my mind, of the minds of each one of us," he lifted his hands, "is peacefulness. Tranquility. And as you abide in this pristine mind, the calmness deepens into an abiding state of bliss.

"Once you have tasted this, even for a moment, you want to go back to it. And the more you can stabilize this experience, the more certain you become that this very primordial consciousness is what you truly are. Not a conglomeration of ideas, that arise and pass, about some fictitious self. Not a self which is constantly changing as we go through life. No, we experience something more subtle, without ego or identity, but which is boundless and benevolent and blissful. And which is reality itself! Just as the renowned Maitripa told his student Marpa:

Generally all phenomena are mind itself.
Your guru arises from this very mind.
There is nothing other than mind.
Whatever appears is all the nature of mind,
Even that is primordially unestablished."

For the longest time everyone in the room was perfectly quiet, wrapped up in the words of Maitripa, or in the presence of Rinpoche. Or was one only a manifestation of the other? Using concepts, Rinpoche had somehow communicated a wisdom, a sensation beyond concepts. And even though none of us may have been able to repeat his meaning or even explain what he'd said, we nevertheless **felt** it as a transcendental reality, an oceanic and pervasive joy that rippled throughout space, connecting us all in intangible and heartfelt waves of benevolence.

I was returned home, not very late, just as Zahra had promised. Making my way through the ground-floor window, along the short corridor and past the larder, I was instantly reminded that this was where I'd last seen the tabby cat shut in a bird cage. But cage and tabby were no longer there.

I headed upstairs and into our apartment, in darkness on account of His Holiness still attending examinations across the courtyard at the monastery. After a few laps of water, I made my way to the sill from where I could observe all the nocturnal comings and goings—including the Dalai Lama's return home, which followed soon after.

We hadn't seen each other since before that afternoon's drama. I wondered if anyone had told him about it. I didn't wonder for long, however. As soon as he stepped into the room, he came over to sit beside me in the darkness, just the way I liked it.

"I heard about today," he reached out, stroking my neck. "How upsetting for you! They tell me this other cat has been around here for a while. Fortunately, Oliver has a very kind heart.

"You know what it's like, don't you Snow Lion? To be without a home. To be without food. To be mistreated."

Until that moment, I had not for one moment thought of the tabby in any way resembling me. Arriving home that afternoon, I'd discovered an interloper. A vicious ambusher. A brute who had invaded my home. But His Holiness was revealing a starkly different version of the tabby. One which likened him to me, the tiny scrap of kittenhood he had rescued from the streets of New Delhi. A version which demanded compassion.

I remembered being startled to see the tabby cowering in the bird cage. Just as I suddenly recollected the very different state of mind with which I'd left the nursing home that afternoon, believing that I'd left all egotistical constraints behind me. Imagining myself to have somehow transcended all self-centeredness. What a rude awakening!

"We all want food and a place to be safe, not so?" The Dalai Lama leaned over me. "We all wish to give and receive love."

These were among the first words I'd ever heard His Holiness speak, seven years ago in this very room. And yet all this time later, I had still to learn the meaning of the words. What I instantly understood in that moment, however, was that the version of the beings we saw in the world around us was as much a reflection of our own mind, as it was of them. And that the more our mind was filled with thoughts of self and our own needs and wishes, the less space and compassion there was for others—and the less happy we would be. Conrad, obsessed with thoughts of his own guilt, had lived a life of miserable self-absorption for the past five years, until Franc had shown him a way out of his self-induced mental prison.

"It is hard to develop heartfelt compassion, to experience true benevolence, if we don't have at least some understanding of sunyata." As was so often the case, the Dalai Lama was once again responding directly to my own thoughts. "If we are fooled by appearances, if we never question the nature of self, well then, we are doomed to remain victims of minds which are the size of sesame seeds.

"But when we let go of this preoccupation, even just a little," he drew himself up beside me as he took in a deep breath and broadened his shoulders, "there is space. Lightness. We can take steps to fulfill our true potential as enlightened beings."

In the deepening night, sharing a moment as we had on many evenings in the past, we looked across the lamp-lit courtyard to where orange squares of light, the curtained windows of the monks' residence, turned to darkness. Then the lights illuminating the auspicious symbols and sacred objects around the temple, each in a particular sequence, also began to be switched off.

"Letting go," the Dalai Lama said, seeming to refer to not only what he'd been saying, but also to what was happening around us. "One by one, all is letting go. If we wish to be happy, we let go of our delusions—**renunciation**. If we wish to fulfill our true purpose, to experience ultimate wellbeing, we let go of our preoccupation with ourselves—**bodhicitta**. And if we wish to act in accordance with reality, we let go of illusions about the way that things exist—**sunyata**."

How wonderful, I thought, that His Holiness could express such profound truths with such exquisite simplicity. In those three sentences he had summarized the first three paws of spiritual success.

There was a fourth, of course. But it had been a long day and it was getting late. Finally, as the lotus bud flicked from gold into shadow, our room fell into darkness too. Through the window, a cool breeze brought the uplifting freshness of Himalayan pine.

A novice monk hurried in sandaled feet across the courtyard to his room, a shadow in the moonlight. "*Om mani padme hum!*" his treble voice carried through the coolness of the night.

"*Om mani padme hum,*" echoed the Dalai Lama in warm benediction.

CHAPTER SEVEN

You know that feeling you get, dear reader, when you sense that something's in the air—but you're not sure exactly what? Maybe you feel a tingle in the whiskers. A twitch about the ears. An awareness that can't be put into words, but that's every bit as obvious as if someone was wandering around with a megaphone making an announcement—only in a foreign language.

Well, that's how things seemed to me down at The Himalaya Book Café. All kinds of things. It was as if, on some unknown, subterranean level there had been a shifting of tectonic plates. A change heralding all manner of possibilities and adventures new.

I became aware, for example, that Serena's program to give teenagers computer skills and help find them jobs had received some kind of official recognition. She had mentioned it to

Bronnie one afternoon, as they'd taken a tea break on the sofa behind me. With the spice pack distribution deal taking off, she'd be able to expand the program to be bigger than ever. **That** was a far greater cause of satisfaction than bureaucratic approval, she'd told Bronnie. All the same, a pat on the back from the government was nice to get.

Several days later, Franc emerged from the manager's office with a piece of paper in his hand. "Have you seen this?" he asked, showing Sam.

"Bronnie said something." He scanned the letter before his eyebrows shot up. "She didn't say anything about …"

"Typical Serena to downplay things," said Franc.

"Probably doesn't want to make a fuss," suggested Sam.

Franc stared into mid-distance for a few moments, his mind evidently elsewhere. "Perhaps we should make a fuss for her," he said, enigmatically.

Later, I heard him on the phone to Sid. The matter of the award was being discussed, along with Serena's reticence about making a big deal of it. Evidently, the two men were in agreement about what was to follow. But I didn't get to hear what arrangements were being planned; Franc closed the office door and spent the rest of the afternoon making a series of phone calls, emerging only from time to time with a glint of excitement in his eyes. Once, I heard him use the word 'bodyguards'.

That wasn't all. Zahra, home from school for the holidays, was coming into the café regularly to help Serena with the spice pack business, with operations run from the offices upstairs.

Which meant, as far as Zahra was concerned, that I must move upstairs too. Picking me up from the magazine rack and clutching me to her chest, she'd carry me up to the desk where she worked, on which she had carefully arranged a fleece blanket. That's where I'd pass the next few hours with my paws tucked under me, watching her very closely—between cuddles and catnaps.

Even though the actual amount of time I spent upstairs wasn't long, there was something very special about spending time with Zahra. A feeling of connection that had a feeling all of its own and which, while delightfully fresh and different, also had the sense of a prelude. A preface. A harbinger of things to come.

What's more, over the past weeks I had noticed a developing liaison between Angela, the new bookstore assistant from Vancouver, and Conrad. It had begun with earnest discussions at the bookshelves: Conrad quizzing Angela for recommendations on travel guides to the local area, and Angela recommending illustrated guides to a variety of mountain hikes—a pursuit, as it turned out, the two of them had in common.

Then one day, instead of standing in the bookstore, they shared one of the restaurant banquettes—the one closest the magazine rack. Since he'd arrived in Dharamshala a couple of months ago, Conrad had been a regular, lone figure at The Himalaya Book Café. Whether reading a book or working on a laptop, there had always been an air of solitariness about him, as if he were surrounded by invisible defenses that held others at bay.

After the encounter with Franc under the cedar tree, however, that had changed. There was a new lightness about him, and an openness. A willingness to engage. This was the first time I'd seen him with a girl, and their conversation was animated and engaged. Angela's pale cheeks were pinker than usual, as she listened attentively to Conrad, brushing her hair back from her face as she gazed into his hazel eyes and studied his dark, chiseled features intently. During the course of their coffee, they moved from deep and meaningful to laughing out loud. I observed a few pauses when they just sat quietly, looking into each other's eyes. Smiling.

When they got up, Conrad touched his right shoulder, saying something about a tightness. That was when Angela suggested he try yoga that evening. She had been attending sessions regularly with Serena over the past few weeks.

"You think it will make a difference?" asked Conrad.

"It might," said Angela.

"I heard that the teacher was away traveling."

"Yes, Ludo's been back in Germany for nearly two months. Loving it, apparently. But some of his senior students are taking classes. And you should see the studio. It has the most amazing view!"

"I thought you were supposed to concentrate on your posture when you do yoga?" he challenged her with a smile. "No distractions."

"True," she agreed, eyes sparkling. "But some distractions are more welcome than others."

With His Holiness addressing a humanitarian conference in New Delhi and not due back till later that night, I decided to go to yoga myself. Perched on my wooden stool at the back of the class, I watched the group of students make their way through the long-familiar sequence of asanas, accompanied by a soundtrack of meditative sitar music, with the rising, soulful cadences of an Indian prayer.

Since Ludo had returned to Germany, several of the more senior students had taken it in turns to lead the group. Tonight was Ewing's turn, and although he progressed smoothly through the postures with flexibility and strength—and some humor when we nearly fell out of his Half Moon pose—there was a very different feeling in the room to when Ludo was in charge. A different energy. A sense of purpose that was missing since he had left.

Ludo's absence had taken its toll on class sizes, especially in the past few weeks. Before Ludo had left, it had been usual for around 25 students to attend. I'd heard Serena talk about how the number had fallen to around half that in recent weeks. On that evening there were just nine, including Angela and first-timer Conrad.

So the timing of what happened next was unfortunate. It occurred at the end of the class, after students had been lying in Shavasana—the pose of the corpse—for about ten minutes. Instead of the gentle soundtrack, an alert began to sound, with rising insistence. Ewing got up and went over to a laptop, plugged into the sound system. The alert was getting louder, and it took him a few seconds to work out what was happening.

"It's Ludo!" he announced, "Calling online!"

The students started getting up from the floor, as Ludo's voice boomed through the sound system. "I wanted to know how class went this evening?" he asked, in that distinctive, Teutonic voice. It was as clear as if he were in the room himself.

There was mischief in his tone, an acknowledgement of the surprise nature of his call. Although there had been a few email exchanges, this was the first time he had phoned since he'd left.

Students were gathering around the computer, waving at the camera. "Hi Ludo!" Serena leaned towards the screen, before Franc nodded, hands at his heart. The others chorused their 'hellos' and 'namastes'.

Ewing reprized how he'd almost toppled over during *Ardha Chandrasana* to further amusement, before Serena told Ludo how wonderful Ewing's choice of 'chakra rebalancing' music had been. The mood was lighthearted, as they asked Ludo about his time in Germany.

Ludo, it seemed, had been immersing himself in the land of his birth, his family and very longstanding friends from childhood. But his thoughts were refocusing again on the Himalayas, and he planned to return in two weeks' time.

Through the speakers, I heard him ask for Sukie who, Ewing had to tell him, wasn't at class that night. Nor was Merrilee, who had occupied the mat beside Sukie for years. Ludo asked after Carlos and Jordan, two other regulars, to be told that they were also absent. Then he instructed Ewing to scan the camera, so that he could see who **had** come to class.

"There are nine of us," Ewing told him.

"Including Conrad, who has joined us from Switzerland," Serena tried to be positive.

For a moment I caught sight of Ludo's face on the computer screen. If he was troubled by what he'd just learnt, he didn't show it. Looking his usual tanned and relaxed self, even more so, he communicated a sense of poised equanimity, despite appearing from halfway around the world and through the medium of a computer screen. He told his students that he would be returning soon. The call ended a short while later with him promising, somewhat mysteriously, that when he returned he was bringing 'a surprise' with him.

Later the group gathered on the usual assortment of cushions, bean bags and rugs on the balcony, to watch the sun set over the Himalayas. Zahra, who had been coming to classes since getting home for the holidays, found a spot between Sid and Serena. Without needing to think, I nestled against her legs, cozy in the company of my favorite family.

Serena looked around the group with a pensive expression. "Poor Ludo. That really **wasn't** what I'd have wanted for him."

She reached down to stroke me.

"Only nine of us, you mean?" queried Ewing.

She nodded.

Then Angela observed, "He didn't seem too worried."

After a pause, Sid responded, "Ludo is a master of equanimity. Even when the studio caught fire—remember, years ago? He still kept his cool."

"A fire?" asked Angela.

"Right here," Serena shuddered. "On the balcony. Fortunately HHC gave us a warning, so we could take early action. It could have been far worse otherwise."

All gazes turned to me.

I looked around at the eyes of Sid and Serena, of Ewing and Franc and the other students, old and new, and I suddenly realized how very long some of us had been coming to this special place and what memories we shared.

"The last time we sat on this balcony with Ludo," Serena returned us to the present, "he was wondering what would happen to the studio in the long term."

"It was very poignant," said Sid. "He spoke of the need to let go. He wondered what would happen to the studio when he finally leaves us forever."

At that moment a cloud appeared on the horizon, obscuring the sun, at the same time as a chill wind blew up the Kangra valley. Goosebumps appeared on Zahra's bare arms.

"What happened tonight," said Serena, "may have provided an answer."

For a moment, the students sipped their beakers of green tea in silence. Then Franc said contemplatively, "One thing is for sure—it shows the importance of the guru."

There were murmurs of agreement before Sid added, "The source of all realizations."

"The foundation of our practice," agreed Franc.

Conrad glanced from one man to the other before asking, "You are talking about more than yoga, yes?"

"Any skills-based learning," said Franc. "And, of course, Dharma practice as well as yoga."

"When you say "guru"," Angela wanted to be clear, "is this different from being an ordinary teacher?"

Franc nodded. "Teachers at school and lecturers at university, they communicate information. They help us understand a subject, work things out in our minds, make sense of things. That's all about transferring knowledge.

"Wisdom is different. It involves the transmission of insights that have the capacity to change us. Only when we understand an insight deeply enough can it create change. At that point, knowledge becomes wisdom." Franc glanced at some of the long-term students for support. "Would you agree?"

The others were nodding. Sid added, "The guru is the embodiment of wisdom. Every action of his body, speech and mind are the expression of wisdom."

"What you're saying," Conrad wanted to clarify, "is that a guru doesn't just explain things. He shows you how it's done. He walks the talk."

There were murmurs of agreement before Serena said, "And there's even more to it. Just look," she gestured around the balcony. "Nine of us. I'm not blaming anyone who isn't here for not coming. The point is, it's not the same without Ludo."

There were murmurs of agreement.

I instantly thought about the windowsill in the Dalai Lama's empty residence. It wasn't the same without him either. Which was why I was at yoga.

"A guru does more than explain and embody," continued Serena. "He also motivates and inspires."

"Like a personal trainer?" offered Conrad.

"Good example!" said Franc.

Up above us, like old friends and guardians nestling around our tiny group, the mountains glowed a deep and munificent orange, so that slanting rays rippled across the deepening evening, lighting up our balcony in an ever-shifting, ethereal dance.

"In the Himalayas," observed Sid, "it is believed that the connection between guru and student is the most important of our lives. Certainly more important than **what** you know, and even what you believe or practice. Especially in spiritual development, what matters more than anything is the direct transmission between teacher and student. Between the realized master and the initiate. It is something that occurs at a level beyond words." He brought his hands together at his heart. "There is ..." he shrugged, searching for expression, "how to put it, a knowingness, an understanding, communicated with such power, that the student no longer has any doubt about ultimate reality embodied by the teacher. Sometimes there can be a radiantly blissful feeling. The student may catch a glimpse, perhaps for the first time, of how it feels to be totally accepted. To experience pure love."

The others were watching Sid right now with intensity as if, at that very minute, he was undertaking exactly such a transmission himself. Gazing at her father adoringly, Zahra leaned over, resting her head briefly against his shoulder.

Sid looked about their faces with wry smile, "We are talking about things that are noetic."

"Something we understand without words?" queried Zahra, nuzzling against his shoulder.

Her father nodded.

"I've heard it said," Ewing commented, "that the guru is like a magnifying glass. Buddha gave 84,000 teachings, but which ones are relevant to you or me? What particular mental obstacles do we have? The idea is that the guru focuses on those teachings and practices relevant to us."

"Kinder than Buddha himself," responded Serena.

"Kinder than Buddha?" Angela sounded surprised. "Isn't that a bit … irreverent?"

Serena was shaking her head. "The historical Buddha, Shakyamuni, isn't physically here today to help us. But our teachers are. They are the ones who are showing us greater kindness by teaching us how to bring an end to dissatisfaction, and how to attain enduring wellbeing. Which is why you can say they are kinder than Buddha."

As Angela digested this, Franc chipped in, "There's even the phrase: *No guru, no Buddha.*"

Serena nodded.

"Most of what we know about Buddha," continued Franc, "comes from our teacher. Whatever connection we feel to the practices comes from the teacher. There are quite a few stories about this. Like the time that Naropa, who was this amazing yogi and teacher, created a manifestation of a deity called Hevajra in the sky, and woke his student Marpa to see. Naropa asked Marpa who he was going to prostrate to first: Hevajra, as the deity; or him, as his guru. Marpa chose Hevajra, thinking he could see Naropa any time he liked. But afterwards Naropa corrected him, pointing out that without the guru there is no Buddha."

For a few moments, the group reflected on this story before Zahra asked Sid, "Don't you always say, Daddy, that the guru's mind and the Buddha's mind are the same. The guru is like the Buddha?"

Sid nodded. "It is useful to think like that. Not for our guru's sake, but for our own. Our gurus don't care what we think of them—they are beyond that. But for our own sake, when we hold someone in very high esteem, we place great value on what they say to us. We derive maximum value from our relationship when we take their advice to heart."

The golden rivers pouring down the mountain peaks had burnished to deep red, as the sun's rays dipped over the far horizon. Down on the balcony, our little group was held together in their contemplation of this evening's unexpected lesson about the importance of the guru. A lesson that had arisen because of Ludo's absence, and was made all the more relevant by his unexpected call.

"The stories told about gurus and their students—they sound really wonderful," said Conrad. "Like student and teacher were so close. But is it really possible to be that way today? Especially for us Westerners, who are not used to that way of thinking? When I think about teachers like Geshe Wangpo—I think he is wonderful, don't get me wrong. But he is so ... remote. He is Tibetan. I am Swiss. Even if he were willing to have me as a student, I wonder if I could ever feel that connection you talk about?"

Sid reached over and gave his shoulder a squeeze. "It's good to be honest. And you should be in no rush to choose a teacher. Just because others want this person or that person for their guru doesn't mean that you have to."

"At school," Ewing recollected, "we had this physics teacher, Dr Stevens, the most highly qualified member of staff. I was in his class. But despite his academic achievements, I didn't get anywhere as his pupil. Dr Stevens had a brilliant mind and loved exploring quantum puzzles and elaborate calculations. The kids who were good at science thought he was great. I didn't. He skated over the basics so quickly that I didn't have time to pick them up. Then when some of us explained the problems we were having, he just couldn't see them. He didn't understand why we couldn't understand, because it was all so obvious to him.

"Fortunately for us, he was replaced by Mr. Bell, who didn't have a physics degree but did know the problems we faced, because he had faced them too. He was a much better teacher for me. And I think it's the same with the Dharma. The right guru for us isn't necessarily the one who is generally regarded as brilliant, or who has the most dazzling academic reputation."

"There are instructions about what to look for in a teacher," proffered Serena. "Certain qualities they should have. Like you say, Ewing, it's not all about qualifications. And our guru doesn't have to be the most famous, or charismatic. The one who constantly flies round the world giving blessings here and initiations there."

"It may be hard even getting to spend time with such a lama," concurred Franc, "let alone connect to him or her."

"That special connection …" from across the balcony, Conrad looked from Serena to Sid with an intense expression. "It must be wonderful to meet the right person. To recognize this person as someone very special."

"Oh, yes!" chimed Angela, glancing at Conrad and meeting his eyes, before glancing away as though suddenly aware of the double meaning in her exclamation. Even in the deepening shadows, there was no missing the darkening of her face.

"It is wonderful," Sid spoke quickly, trying to spare her further blushes. "Which is why finding our guru is so important. The start of our Dharma journey, you might say. And you are right to use the word "recognize". In Buddhism, we believe that once a guru has accepted you as a student, it is his responsibility—or hers—to guide you to enlightenment, no matter how many lifetimes that takes."

"So the guru may have been your guru before?" Conrad's eyes were alight.

"Exactly," nodded Sid.

"Many lives, many masters—or maybe just the one," observed Ewing, wryly.

"I never realized," Conrad was shaking his head, "how important the guru is."

Franc, who had been leaning against a bolster for a while, eyes shut as he listened to the conversation around him, spoke with a simplicity that evidently came from deep conviction. "In the Dharma," he said, "guru is everything, and everything is guru. The guru is renunciation, because it is he who shows us that our problems are not out there in the world, but in our minds—where we can do something about them. The guru is bodhicitta, because it is he who shows us that the path to enlightenment is by helping others achieve their highest potential. You may say he is the **embodiment** of bodhicitta. And the guru is sunyata, because when we meditate in his presence, and our mind meets with his, we experience non-duality directly for ourselves. We transcend the experience of outer and inner, of self and other; and for a while we may abide in the boundless peace which is his Buddha nature, and ours too."

In the shadows of dusk, the ice caps of the mountains softened to the faintest pink. Franc's words sounded with such clarity, and came from a place of such heartwarming truth, that Serena reached over towards him and squeezed his hand. No need for words.

At that moment, Zahra turned to look directly at Serena, asking her with powerful, teenage curiosity, unfettered by politeness: "What's the best thing the guru has done for you, Serena?"

It was a good question. Asked with clarity. One that deserved an answer.

And it was only after a pause that Serena felt able to respond: "Faith," she said. "Faith, not in an external power or belief system, but in myself. Faith that, like the guru, I have all I need right here," she touched her heart. "I only need to develop it."

After the balcony session ended, Serena, Sid and Zahra stayed at the studio to help Ewing tidy up and vacuum—my least favorite of domestic activities. Do you, dear reader, know of any cat that **does** enjoy the infernal racket of the vacuum cleaner?!

Stepping out of The Downward Dog School of Yoga to make my way home, I found myself a short distance behind Conrad and Angela. In the twilight, I heard them talking and laughing softly, Angela's feminine voice and Conrad's bass tones rising and falling. Arms by their sides, perhaps it was the effects of yoga—the lengthening and stretching, making their arms and wrists more supple—or could it have been for some other reason that the backs of their hands kept meeting and brushing together?

At the bottom of the road leading to the yoga studio, we arrived at a T-junction; the two of them turned left, and I turned right towards Namgyal Monastery. I paused. A group of cyclists was hurtling round the corner from the right hand side in a flurry of raised voices and whirring tires, obscuring Angela and Conrad from view.

When the cyclists had passed, the two of them had walked further down the street and were standing, looking in a shop window together. Holding hands.

Perhaps after all the talk in recent weeks, letting go of thoughts was a practice with which I was becoming more familiar. Maybe it was the inspiration of Yogi Tarchin, when he'd spoken in the tower room about abiding in the true nature of consciousness. Or perhaps it was something Franc had just said about the meeting of minds. For whatever reason, as I made my way back towards the gates of Namgyal Monastery, instead of following my habitual path home, I felt guided by an impulse to do something different. One that didn't seem to have anything to do with ideas of my own, because I wasn't actively thinking. I was just being in the evening, and the origins of what happened were impossible to describe. Perhaps you could say it was an awareness? A sense of something. An inkling I allowed to become manifest.

I carried on further up the road. Along to the garden, which I rarely visited at night and was now silent, and across the lawn next to the unoccupied bench. And without even pausing for the catnip, I climbed through the rockery and crossed to the veranda of the nursing home. It was still early evening, but the veranda was empty, the sliding doors closed and the curtains drawn.

Finding nowhere to enter, I headed round the side of the building, making my way on the pavers that skirted it, until I found myself at the front. This was not somewhere I'd ventured before. At a glance I took in the empty parking bays and worn bitumen, the whitewashed front of the building with its bright lights. Most importantly, the front door leading to a reception area. It was open.

I made my way inside. There was no-one at reception, but I could hear sounds of voices and scraping of cutlery somewhere inside, as meals were being eaten. Carrying on, I ventured down a corridor, unfamiliar with the layout of the place, but guided by the same homing instinct that had led me to this destination once before, though from a different starting point.

Hilda's room had just a single, warm lamp in the corner, and her bed was still on the far side of the room next to the windows. The curtains remained undrawn—perhaps they had been left open so she could enjoy that evening's sunset?

She lay motionless and alone in the shadows next to the dark window. Heading towards her, I was able to hop first onto a visitor's chair, then to the windowsill, before taking a final leap onto her bed. Being a cat of uncertain poise, I landed with an unceremonious thump next to her feet. But if she felt any movement, she didn't react.

She lay with her head propped on a pillow and tilted to the right, eyes closed, face very pale and only the subtlest of movement in the breathing tubes that led into her nose. Her body seemed to have shrunken even more, to the size of a child. Her right arm was draped outside the covers and it was there that I ventured, carefully stepping between her torso and arm. Finding a place to settle near her elbow, I circled, kneading the bedlinen before lowering myself, so she could feel the warmth of me on her arm, the touch of my coat against her fingertips.

I began to purr. As I did, I fixed my sapphire-blue gaze on her face. And I knew, beyond any doubt, what had brought me to her. That sixth sense, that guiding impulse was one I hadn't questioned. I had followed it and now the only thing of importance was to communicate that she was not alone. She may have to undertake the next, vital transition by herself, but she would be doing so from a place of compassion, with a presence of loving kindness.

It would have been nice for me if she had been able to open her eyes, one last time. But she didn't have the energy—and besides, this wasn't about me. In those still and sacred moments with just the two of us, the sounds of the nursing home in the distance belonging to a different world, she did acknowledge my presence with a gentleness. For just a moment, I felt the fingers of her right hand close around my furry softness. Then a short while later, a twitch on her lips as she smiled.

It was enough. The connection was definite—she knew I was with her. And my purring surged as I felt her own energy diminish, like the dwindling flame of a candle, flickering smaller and with less certainty during each tentative breath.

I have heard stories about the death rattle, which some people make before they die. With Hilda, it wasn't like that. Instead there was a gradual slowing. A gentle withdrawal from an already fragile presence, one that felt entirely natural. The very slight movement in her breathing tubes became all the more subtle, before finally ceasing altogether.

In Tibetan Buddhism, physical death is not the end of the process. All bodily functions have closed down, but consciousness remains in the body for a while; in the ordinary person, anywhere from a few moments to much longer. During this time, mental activity goes through a process of dissolution, different elements of consciousness close down, one by one, until only a very subtle consciousness remains at the heart.

All the while this was happening I continued to purr, the vibrations carrying my wish for her deepest happiness, for her to move onto a more wonderful experience of reality. Ultimately, for her to become enlightened.

As the lamas so often say, the state of mind you have at the time you die can be highly significant in determining what karmas ripen, to propel you into the future. For this reason, our final moments of consciousness are considered to be among the most significant of our entire life. The clutch of Hilda's hand and the smile on her face signaled that she'd had at least some contentment, some peace at her very end. And from what I sensed about Hilda, those signals pointed to a tranquility and gratitude that was deeply felt.

I don't know how long I remained with Hilda. And whether it was my imagination or something different, dear reader, I cannot say. But after some minutes had passed in that peaceful bubble that Hilda and I occupied—a place where open minds and hearts could still make contact, if only in the most elemental way—I felt a shift of energy. A release.

There was a sense that she had left her body and, along with it, all the limitations she'd had to endure. Restrictions so suffocating that for a very long time she hadn't even been able to breathe without support. In an instant, she was gone.

Soon afterwards, I decided to go too. Rising from her bed, I hopped to sill, then chair, then floor, and I headed back across the room. Along the corridor outside and through reception— still deserted. Out into the night, using the pavers around the building to return me to the veranda.

The whole place was in darkness, but it was a cloudless night and the moon and stars cast the rockery in an ethereal light, washing the boulders a mysterious white, and making the agapanthus leaves ripple as waves of silver in the evening breeze. Like most cats, I am a creature of the night. The moonlit hours whisper to me of secrets that can't be shared during the hours of broad daylight. In some significant way, I felt closer to the world of spirit, to a time of revelation, of intuition and wonder.

Pushing my way through the darkness between the starlit stems, I emerged on the other side of the flowerbed. Unlike on my way to see Hilda, the bench seat was no longer unoccupied, the garden no longer silent. Conrad and Angela sat under the boughs of the cedar tree, in each other's arms and kissing. Utterly lost to one another, they paid me no attention as I emerged from the flower bed and crossed the lawn a short distance away. Indeed, I could have manifest not as one, but as eight full-sized snow lions, the kind that support the thrones of the largest Buddha statues in temples throughout the Himalayas—two at each corner—and they still wouldn't have noticed me, so single-minded was their focus.

I found my way to the steps leading down to the road. As I did, I glanced towards the mountains, their frosted peaks looking as though they were suspended, by some magic, in mid-air. From behind me came the breathing of young lovers. Out there, somewhere, the subtle consciousness that had once been at the heart of Hilda, may have been seeking manifestation.

Where would it be drawn? And to whom? What karma had she created that would predispose her to experience a new chapter in a particular realm, or as a particular kind of being? Awakened to elements of the circle of life, I was struck with the infinitude of possibilities, as well as a sense of abiding peace that, beneath the play of ordinary appearances, all was well. As long as we kept on practicing loving kindness and creating the grounds for positive future outcomes, we need have no fear of what might arise.

All the same, as I made my way home, the curious part of me, that inquisitive, self-absorbed part that sought a resolution to all mystery, couldn't help wondering again about the gap in my own, particular circle of life. That interval of decades, between my time as the Dalai Lama's dog in 1960, and my manifestation as his cat, seven years ago.

Where had I gone? To whom had I been connected? Perhaps it was something of the magic of the night, dear reader, but I had a sense that all this would soon be revealed.

It so happened that the vehicle bringing His Holiness back from New Delhi pulled into the gates of Namgyal Monastery around the same time that I was crossing the courtyard. Within moments, the Dalai Lama was stepping out from the car, stretching his legs and back, and coming over to where I was sitting.

"Good evening, my little Snow Lion! How nice to see you!" He bent down to stroke me.

Oliver emerged from the car—they had evidently been traveling together—along with two, large bodyguards.

"Things look so much nicer at night than during the day," he observed, tuning into my own consciousness as he glanced around the familiar courtyard, lit only by the light of the stars and the moon. The temple was in darkness, all the lights both outside and within having been switched off some time ago. Unusually, the temple door had been left open. Through the entrance we could see right down the center, to where lights at the feet of the central Buddha statue were a permanent presence, flickering like candles, a glowing offering to the presence of enlightenment.

It was rare to see the temple like that. In a moment of spontaneity, His Holiness reached down, picked me up, and held me to him as he walked up the steps, kicking off the sandals he was wearing, before venturing inside. Oliver and the bodyguards followed.

For a while, we stood silently at the back, simply taking in our surroundings. The great, painted thangkas had fallen into darkness. The intricate colors and motifs decorating the temple were completely obscured. Our gaze was drawn to the only source of light and the magnificent statue it illuminated, the golden face and blue eyes of Shakyamuni Buddha.

"Now that you know the four aspects of the path," His Holiness whispered in my ear. "Renunciation, bodhicitta, sunyata and guru yoga. Can you see how every Buddha is a visual reminder of them?"

In the Dalai Lama's arms, I gazed at the Buddha, wanting so much to understand what His Holiness meant, but unable to. I still couldn't see four of anything. Unless you counted his four limbs, but I didn't think the Dalai Lama meant that. It was as though he was talking in the riddles of twilight language.

Being held in a person's arms for any length of time made me uncomfortable. Without me needing to ask, His Holiness put me down and I stepped over to the nearest object—a chair. I rubbed my chin then the rest of my body against the chair leg, in a show of affection by proxy. As I did so my tail, which was pointing directly upwards, vibrated in that way we cats do when feeling especially blissful. The Dalai Lama took in the electronic tail quiver and chuckled.

Behind us, the others looked at me too. "Most peculiar cat," observed one of the bodyguards.

"Now, that's a tautology if ever I heard one," quipped Oliver.

"Tautology?" queried His Holiness.

"When you repeat the same thing using different words, like "peculiar" and "cat". All cats are peculiar, aren't they?"

Contemplating me seriously, it was a while before the Dalai Lama nodded, "Yes. Unpredictable. A little bit of a mystery."

Reaching down to stroke me he added, "Which is why we love them so much."

CHAPTER EIGHT

THERE'S A KERNEL OF TRUTH TO BE FOUND IN MANY AN OLD proverb, wouldn't you say, dear reader? Wisdom—not always of the most profound or subtle kind—that can sum up an idea in a single phrase. Which is why I've always wondered about that most cat-centric of proverbs: *Curiosity killed the cat.*

Did it really? Which cat exactly? And why? Has it ever been your experience that a feline you know was led to his or her death by an overly inquisitive nature?

It certainly hasn't been my experience. We cats may be an inquiring lot, as well as a species of risk-takers, but those risks are usually well-calculated, supported by our lithe bodies, athletic prowess and mental perspicacity.

I have to admit, there have been a few close shaves. A couple of episodes in which things could have gone very badly wrong indeed.

One of them came just a few days after my final visit to Hilda. I had made my way down the hill to The Himalaya Book Café early one afternoon, when I found the laundry door ajar. Oh, joy of joys! Oh, wonder of wonders! In all the years I had been coming to the café, there had never been such a lapse. Head Waiter Kusali and his staff were always punctilious about keeping that particular door firmly closed. It was only ever opened to drop a used tablecloth, napkin or other such item into a basket, or to retrieve said basket for washing.

When I say 'laundry', I am repeating the word used by the staff. If you were to visit the café to investigate, you might decide it was a 'cupboard'. Whatever you choose to call it, however, the door that was usually inalterably shut was open that afternoon.

In much the same way as the veranda door of the nursing home had been my entrance to a whole new dimension of experience, would the same be true of the laundry? Might it offer another rabbit hole down which to explore a different and more exotic reality?

Unlike the nursing home, the laundry door hadn't been deliberately left open. And there was just a smidgen of a gap. But enough for a small, furry paw to reach behind and lever wider, creating just sufficient space for a fluffy body to step from the parquet flooring of the café onto the bare concrete within. And with a single, sprightly hop, to launch into a basket laden with tablecloths, which sank delightfully beneath my weight, creating the perfect bed. So pliant were the fabrics and so cushiony, that just kneading them made me feel drowsy. Was it the softness, or the slight tang of that day's lunch menu now permeating the fabrics, that made me so deliciously sleepy?

When one of the waiters launched another tablecloth into the laundry, which settled on top of me like a tepee, perfection was achieved. Within minutes, I was soundly asleep.

You will probably have already predicted, dear reader, that things started to unravel sometime after this. I became aware of movement but wasn't unduly troubled by it. Roused from a deep sleep, I became aware that the pressure on my head was greater than it had been. I wasn't unduly troubled by that either.

It was only after the sudden thud, when I felt my whole body crushed, that I woke right up. And found myself unable to move! Physically oppressed. Squeezed between layers of fabric, a gap between folds of napkins was the only reason I was able to breathe.

There was a sudden crashing sound. One I recognized, but in my befuddled and confused state I couldn't place. The sound of an engine starting. A jolt, followed by ongoing vibrations.

Then I realized where I was. The same ritual was performed every afternoon at The Himalaya Book Café. The linen basket would be taken from the laundry and placed in the back of a car. An additional basket of soiled aprons and kitchen towels would be loaded on top of it. They would be taken to the drycleaners where, from what I'd heard, the contents would be thrown into a large, heated cylinder, reeking with potent chemicals, to be rotated until they were clean.

I meowed. In the confined space and unable to fully inflate my lungs, I wasn't able to make much noise. Plus I had the car engine to compete with. But I tried to make my presence known.

I had no idea who was driving the car, because the staff took it in turns. Some days it was Franc; other days, Serena. Kusali had a driver's license as did Sam, who was also occasionally pressed into service to do the laundry run.

I could feel the car heading around corners and up steep inclines. Whenever we descended a hill, the pressure bearing down was so great it winded me. I had no sense of time. Whenever I was able I made a plaintive noise, hoping to be heard above the racket of the engine, the traffic, and perhaps the car radio.

On and on it went, and I felt more and more distraught.

Then suddenly, we shuddered to a stop and I heard men's voices. A few moments later there was the clunk of a handle being opened and a rocking sensation.

I meowed again, as much as I was able; I knew that whatever sound I was making would be muffled beneath layers of tablecloths and a full hamper of tea towels. There was a violent rocking before the pressure suddenly lessened. Then a lurching movement.

I meowed, plaintively. I could tell the basket was being carried. I could feel the motion as whoever was holding it moved forward, step by step. There were more voices, but I couldn't recognize them. A halt before the basket was put down. Meowing at the top of my lungs, I was aware that the tablecloths and napkins were being removed from above and around me.

Then suddenly, I could see up. "Rinpoche!" Zahra's was the first face I saw. "Oh, my poor baby! I thought I heard something."

I noticed Sam there too—he must have been the one behind the steering wheel. Two men from the laundry were also standing by, evidently about to take the baskets and all they contained.

Zahra quickly lifted me from the basket. "I hope you're okay?" she crooned.

I hoped so too! As she placed me on the ground, like a fragile ornament, I felt myself wobble to a standing position, taking my first breath free from the constraints of a vast pile of dirty washing. Not the steadiest of cats at the best of times, it took me a few moments to adjust to simply being upright in the light, able to fill my lungs.

After a short while, I tried a tentative step. Before taking another one, still very shaky. "Looks like she's okay," observed Sam. "I can take her back to the café, if you like?"

On her haunches beside me, Zahra looked up. "But it's the wrong direction for you, isn't it?"

Sam glanced at his watch, shrugging. "It's not too far."

I met Zahra's concerned expression and meowed pitifully.

Taking in Sam's need to get moving and my own plight, Zahra quickly came to a decision.

"Why don't you drop me off, as planned? I'll take Rinpoche with me."

"You'll be okay with her?"

"Of course," said Zahra. "Serena is coming to collect me in about an hour. It won't be for long and we can keep an eye on her."

"We?" I wondered. Who might that be? But there was no time for conjecture because, decision taken, Zahra picked me up and took me back to the car. This time I sat in the front passenger seat on her lap, as Sam got in beside us and started the engine.

The moment we arrived at the place I knew I had been here before. On one occasion only, with Serena. The Cartrights' house was a rambling old villa not far from Namgyal Monastery, with beautifully tended gardens and old style polished wooden floors, layered with beautifully woven Indian rugs. Zahra knocked on the open wooden door.

A few moments later, Dorothy Cartright appeared at the end of the hallway, a striking woman who held herself with a poised calm. A long-time friend both of Mrs. Trinci and Sid, Dorothy had known Zahra since she was a little girl.

"You've brought the Dalai Lama's Cat with you?" she observed, beckoning Zahra in.

"Long story," Zahra replied. "She stowed away in some laundry hampers we just dropped off. If we hadn't heard her meowing, she could have ended up being dry-cleaned."

"Oh, horrors!" Dorothy raised her hand to her throat.

"Is it okay if I take her in with me?"

"As it happens," Dorothy was leading us down a passage, "I think Yogi Tarchin has quite a soft spot for her."

A short while later, I was following Zahra into his room. The Cartrights had sponsored Yogi Tarchin through many years of retreats, and when he came out of retreat to Dharamshala, he usually stayed with them. His room, at the back of the house, was quite separate and exactly as I remembered it, from the brass doorknob that Zahra turned when summoned, to the temple-like expanse of space as she stepped inside.

Illuminated only by three long narrow windows, through which the afternoon sun glowed a burnished gold, the light in the room felt imbued with the milk and honey of devotional energy. Opposite the door was a day bed on which Rinpoche sat, cross-legged. With his crimson, Nehru-collared shirt, goatee beard and an expression as tranquil as it was ageless, he looked the archetypal guru.

Somewhat self-consciously, Zahra performed three prostrations on the carpet in front of him before meeting his eyes.

He nodded in acknowledgement, then raised his arms, face lighting up in a smile. She hurried over and they embraced warmly. After a while, they broke apart. Rinpoche gestured towards a large, comfortable-looking cushion on the carpet in front of him. Zahra sat down, collecting her thoughts.

As she did, Yogi Tarchin glanced at where I was silently crossing from the door towards Zahra, a glint in his eye. "My dear Zahra," he said. "You have brought someone with you."

She nodded, reaching out to stroke my neck and guide me towards her. "We had a bit of an accident earlier. I thought we'd left her at the café. But that didn't happen."

He nodded in a way that seemed to suggest none of this came as a surprise. "Some of the most intriguing outcomes arise from apparent accidents; is it not so, HHC?" He fixed me with an indulgent smile.

I thought of the 'accident' that had brought His Holiness' car to a halt in New Delhi at the precise moment that two street urchins—who'd spent all day in vain trying to sell me, a mere scrap of a kitten at the time—wrapped me up in newspaper, intending to throw me away as garbage. The 'accident' that had seen Sam Goldberg—a highly knowledgeable young bookseller, but recently made redundant and deeply disheartened—find himself visiting what used to be Franc's Café, at exactly the time that Franc had decided to move into books.

This afternoon's accident, that had brought us together.

We sat in silence for a while, because in the presence of lamas like Yogi Tarchin, the present moment is such a delightful place to be. With a master to draw you gently away from agitation or dullness, into the radiant boundlessness of primordial consciousness, what need is there for anything else?

Sitting together, I felt a strong sense of deja vu, having once followed Serena to this same room in very similar circumstances, for an audience with Rinpoche. Then as now, Yogi Tarchin had only just emerged from a three-year retreat and was staying with the Cartrights. Serena, who had recently arrived back in Dharamshala from Europe, had all sorts of questions about the value of meditation; whether there was a difference between mind and brain; and whether ordinary people were capable of clairvoyance. She had also been burdened by one particular question: would there ever be a man in her life, especially if she made a permanent move back to India?

Yogi Tarchin had offered her hope. Much to her bemusement, he'd suggested she may already have met her future husband. Little had she realized at the time that the tall, quiet man in the back row of her yoga class was, in fact, her soulmate.

That day it was Zahra's turn to ask questions. "There are so many things I want to know," she began, meeting Rinpoche's eyes. "When I'm with Dad and Serena, they want me to keep quiet, like I'm a child."

"Yes, yes," he was nodding. "They wish you to be respectful. Which is right. But you are at an age where you are starting to take responsibility for your own mind."

Zahra absorbed this in silence before saying, somewhat anxiously, "The other night at yoga they were talking about being a student and how important it is to have a teacher."

"The foundation of all realizations," intoned Rinpoche, his voice lifting the energy in the room to an even more rarefied level.

Zahra nodded. "That's exactly what they were saying. What I mean is, is it okay for me to think of you, like, is it alright if …" She was looking at the floor awkwardly. Then taking a deep breath, straightening her shoulders and looking at Rinpoche she said, "What I'd like to ask is—please and very respectfully—will you be my teacher?"

Leaning forward on the day bed, Yogi Tarchin reached out his hands, took hers in his for a few moments and squeezed them. "I have always thought of you as my special heart student," he smiled, before gently letting go.

Zahra was smiling. "Good! So I already am. I didn't know if I was supposed to ask."

Rinpoche's expression was understanding. "The place a teacher occupies in your mind and heart comes from your side, not the teacher's. What people say can sometimes be mere noise," he shrugged. "Sound without meaning. More important is how we feel about our guru here," he touched his heart, "and trying sincerely to embody the teachings."

Zahra was wriggling on her cushion. "They used the words "guru yoga". But that's nothing to do with **yoga** yoga is it? Stretching and postures and all that?"

Yogi Tarchin chuckled. "Not physical yoga, no. Yoga means to unite. To join." He interlaced the fingers of both hands. "It is a Sanskrit word—the English word "yoke" comes from it. In physical yoga, we bring together body and mind. In guru yoga, we bring together our mind with the mind of the guru. Which, importantly, we see as being the same as the mind of a Buddha. It is a way to help us evolve from an ordinary mind, afflicted with karma and delusion, to the consciousness of a Buddha, which is blissful and transcendent, beyond birth and death."

"When you say, bringing together your mind with your teacher's mind, that is something we imagine happening, right?"

"From your side," Rinpoche nodded. "Correct. From the teacher's side, from the Buddha's side, there are powerful and positive beings or energies, who wish to help you. But they can't do it without your openness. Without your wish for it to happen."

Zahra's forehead was lined in concentration. "Just for argument's sake …" she began, before halting.

"Debate is good." Yogi Tarchin encouraged her. "It helps clarify understanding."

"Okay. Just for argument's sake, how can you make something happen just by imagining it? I mean, just because I imagine something happening—like, I don't know, bumping into a famous pop star on the way home today—just 'cos I imagine this, it's not going to make it happen."

Rinpoche moved his head from side to side before saying, "You are right—in the short term. But yoga is a process. Long term. You don't go to one yoga class and come out with a supple and flexible body. You have to keep practicing. You don't meet a famous pop star because you daydream about it for a few minutes.

"But what would happen if, for example, you started to follow that pop star online? You went to every concert, got to know everything about that pop star, shaped your life around the pop star, and constantly thought of ways to connect and become close to the pop star. You did this for years and years with the firm resolve of meeting the pop star. Do you think then, one day, there may be a chance of meeting the pop star—perhaps as head of the pop star's Indian fan club? Perhaps at a charity event supported by the pop star?"

Zahra had been following Rinpoche intently. "I suppose," she nodded.

"Everything begins with **intention**," he told her. "With deciding we want something, and then bringing it together, uniting our actions of body, speech and mind until we get it. Pop star yoga!"

Zahra grinned. "No point going to all that effort just to meet a pop star," she said.

"Exactly! These days you hear a lot about the Law of Attraction. About how you can decide on a goal, visualize the goal in detail, repeat affirmations about the goal, and put the goal at the center of all you do, until it becomes manifest."

"Does it work?" asked Zahra.

"If you practice," said Rinpoche. "But no quick fix. No instant solutions. The problem, these days, is that these teachings are often used for debased purposes. They have been cheapened because of how they are used. They are sold as ways to get money, status, romance. There's nothing wrong with these things, but they are not a true cause of happiness. They have no value beyond this lifetime.

"The best use for these methods is in our practice of Dharma. That is how they evolved. When we begin our journey with renunciation, we accept that our happiness, our wellbeing, is dependent not so much on circumstances, as on our mind. We decide to turn away from the true causes of our unhappiness, which is, say, our attachment or anger, and instead cultivate more beneficial mental states. We take refuge in the Buddha, Dharma and Sangha, yes?"

Zahra was nodding.

"Then we cultivate bodhicitta. We try to recollect our wish to attain enlightenment for the benefit of all beings. We try to embody this in all that we do. But to begin with, becoming a Buddha is just an idea we have about ourselves. An act of imagination. We are not Buddhas. We are just naughty people," Rinpoche's face crinkled as he chuckled, his eyes closing and his laughter infectious as Zahra joined in. Motes of dust danced in the amber light of the afternoon.

"But we have to start somewhere," he continued after a while. "Where you start doesn't matter. It's where you end up that counts. Bodhicitta begins as an act of imagination. So does sunyata wisdom. We can do analysis about the way that things exist. Most useful. But at some point we need to meditate on what it means that all things lack inherent existence. To use our imagination and conceive of what reality may be like, if it is free of independent phenomena. What our mind might be like free of thought. First, we have the imagined, conceptual idea. Then we can have the non-conceptual experience."

As he held Zahra's eyes he told her, "All the way along the path, we use intention and imagination. It's like that with guru yoga, also."

"Did you say we should imagine the guru as being like a Buddha?" asked Zahra.

Yogi Tarchin nodded.

"I've been to a few of Geshe Wangpo's talks, but I don't think I've heard him say that before. Why not?"

A wry smile appeared on Rinpoche's face. "This is a very ... inconvenient subject to teach. Geshe Wangpo has quite a few Westerners come to his talks?"

Zahra nodded.

"Especially for Westerners, they are sometimes nervous about this idea. They think it is like some kind of a cult. An ego thing. Imagine if a lama were to say, "It is best that you think of me as being like a Buddha". Well, some of the students would be saying: "He can't be a Buddha—have you seen his table manners?!" And others would be saying: "What an arrogant monk! Who is he to claim enlightenment?" And so on.

"This is why many lamas tell students to read the texts on this subject and hope they will work it out for themselves. Join the dots. Because you see, thinking your guru is like a Buddha is not for his sake. What you think of him is to do with **your** mind, **your** attitude. The more you are able to think of him as being like a Buddha, the better it is for your own inner development. If you listen to a teaching and think of the lama as being ordinary, you receive ordinary blessings. If you think of the lama as being a Buddha, you receive a Buddha's blessings."

Before him on the carpet, Zahra contemplated this for a while, reaching out to stroke me where I was sitting beside her, paws tucked under and looking up at Rinpoche.

"If the teaching is the same, don't you get the same benefit, whether you hear it from an ordinary lama or from a Buddha?"

Raising his eyebrows, Rinpoche nodded his head. "Good debating skills, Zahra," he congratulated her. "Answer this. If your father tells you something, perhaps something you don't want to hear, what do you say?"

Zahra shrugged her shoulders.

"I think I know." There was a twinkle in Rinpoche's eyes, before he assumed an unexpectedly convincing attitude.

"Whatever?" he mimicked, in an obstinate voice.

Zahra giggled self-consciously.

"Something like that?" He leaned back.

She nodded.

"Now. What if you went to see His Holiness the Dalai Lama, and he told you exactly the same thing. Would you say "whatever"?" He repeated the impersonation.

"Course not!" she protested.

As the glow in the room mellowed and softened, its intensity beginning to wane, Yogi Tarchin left it to Zahra to work through the implications of what she'd just confirmed. Her discovery that the power of words came less from the words themselves, than from the person who spoke them. And that who spoke them, lama or Buddha, was at least partly for us to decide.

Then Zahra asked him, "When you say "blessings", what do you mean?"

"A blessing is the capacity to change," he told her simply. "When we are blessed, we receive the inspiration, the energy, the will to transform our experience of reality in some way, from ordinary to transcendental."

"Is that when you can use your dream body to go anywhere you like in your sleep? Or heal people by saying mantras, or be completely clairvoyant?"

Rinpoche chuckled. "You are talking about very advanced practices. In the Dharma we have the sutra path, which are the core teachings. Only when we are very familiar with these, and have integrated them into our lives, can we receive initiations from our guru to practice highest yoga tantra."

Rolling onto my side, I gave all four paws a tremulous stretch, yawning widely. Zahra stroked my tummy and I luxuriated in the sensation of her fingernails, as they traced their way down my body, through my thick fur coat. Then, curling up beside her, head upside down, I assumed the pose of the croissant.

Although spontaneous, my movement reflected a shift in the room. Specifically, Zara's wish to ask Yogi Tarchin questions of a more personal nature.

"These past few years," she began tentatively. "I keep having questions about my mother. Dad has moved on with his life, and I love Serena. She's wonderful! All the same, I keep coming back to Mummy and what happened to her. That's why I asked you about her when you came round for dinner."

Rinpoche nodded.

"And you said it's not always possible to be born a human with wealth and privilege."

"Yes."

"I've been thinking, does that mean she could have been reborn as someone poor, perhaps?"

Rinpoche met her earnest expression steadily. "The Buddha himself gave an example of how rare it is to be born human," he told her.

"Most of the time we think of ourselves as ordinary. Normal. But this is a mistake. Just to be born human is exceptional. The Buddha's example was of a blind, crippled turtle that comes to the surface of the ocean every hundred years, and just happens to stick its neck through a golden ring floating on the surface. The golden ring symbolizes a life of leisure and fortune—like the one we enjoy.

"When we look around the world, we know there are seven billion humans and countless trillions of birds, animals and fish. The chance of being born human is actually very small. Sadly, most humans don't recognize what this means. They don't understand how we have an extraordinary opportunity to develop our minds, and escape the constant cycle of birth, aging, death and rebirth. And that if we don't make the most of this precious opportunity, it may be a long time before it comes again."

"What is the cause of human rebirth, Rinpoche?"

"Virtue."

"So if you are a virtuous person, coming back as a human in your next life is …?"

"More likely," he nodded. Before regarding her with an expression of profound compassion. "The karma that ripens at the time we die can also have a big impact."

"Which is why it's best to die with a peaceful mind."

He nodded.

"Not like Mummy in a car accident?"

Shanti had died when her car had plunged over the side of a cliff.

"Time can be experienced very differently in moments like that. It can stretch out dramatically compared to usual. So even in a car accident—we cannot say what a person's experience of that moment may have been. We shouldn't jump to conclusions."

"I've heard that there are different kinds of karma affecting rebirth," said Zahra. "Can you tell me about them?"

"There is throwing karma and finishing karma," said Yogi Tarchin. "Throwing karma is what propels us into a life form—as a human being, say, or a bird. Finishing karma is the kind of life we will have as that human or bird. Very good finishing karma could see us born into a family of affluent Dharma practitioners. With very bad finishing karma, we may end up as very poor people in a war zone, only able to focus on survival and our next meal."

"So, if Mummy didn't have the throwing karma to be reborn as a human being," Zahra was working this through. "She could perhaps have had the throwing karma to be an animal of some kind. Maybe with good finishing karma. Like a pet?"

"Pets who enjoy good homes have very good karma," agreed Rinpoche. "They don't have to worry much about safety or food. They can give and receive affection. If they hear mantras very often and see auspicious symbols and statues, their karma is affected. It could be that they are just using up some negative karma, before being able to continue on the path to enlightenment."

"I've heard that Mummy was very devoted to the Dalai Lama."

"I never met her," said Yogi Tarchin. "But I have heard the same."

"And devoted to Daddy, of course."

Rinpoche leaned forward on the day bed and fixed her with a surprisingly forceful expression. "And to you," he said, in a tone of voice that both commanded attention to what he had just said, and also seemed to come as his final words on the subject. Words which, at that moment, seemed pointed to a conclusion so self-evident that Zahra couldn't avoid it.

Nor could I! Uncurling myself with unusual alacrity, I sat up, gazing from Rinpoche to Zahra, my eyes meeting first his and then hers. Those few moments were, quite simply, among the most extraordinary of my life.

What had been revealed was so amazing, but also so self-evident, there could be no doubting it. In the late afternoon, although the glow of the sun had faded and the corners of the room were fading into shadow, sitting with Zahra at the feet of Rinpoche was like being at the center of a vortex of love and light, of joy and transcendence, of a knowingness which couldn't be put into words—and didn't need to be.

Leaning over, Zahra touched her forehead to mine, then ran her hands down both sides of me. Her breathing shaky, she gulped for air and I felt her tears falling onto my coat.

"You've always been so special to me." She gave voice to exactly my own thoughts. "Now I know why."

It was early evening when Serena collected Zahra and me from the Cartrights. She was soon told the story of the laundry basket and how, that afternoon, I had become an unwitting stowaway. Instead of driving directly home with Zahra, she drove to Namgyal Monastery, with me perched in the front on Zahra's lap.

Once there, we went upstairs and Tenzin immediately showed us through to where His Holiness and Oliver were sitting at a desk, working on a translation. Returned to my familiar surroundings, I crossed over to the windowsill, while Serena briefly recounted that afternoon's drama.

"It seems that the laundry door at the café was left open today, which has never happened in the past," she explained.

"I am very grateful to you, Zahra," His Holiness bowed his head. "If you hadn't heard her meowing at the laundry …"

They all glanced towards me before Serena said, "Curiosity killed the cat. Isn't that the old saying?"

"It is a saying," confirmed Oliver, "and the one generally used these days. But it's not the original saying used by the likes of Shakespeare."

"Go on?" prompted Tenzin, ever the Anglophile.

"The original proverb was much more like Buddhism actually," said His Holiness' translator. "*Care killed the cat, but satisfaction brought it back.* Care meant worry or anxiety."

"A message about cultivating contentment," commented the Dalai Lama.

"Exactly," Oliver nodded.

"Well, I hope HHC is satisfied," said Serena.

"Oh, I'm sure she is," said Zahra emphatically. "She lives with her guru."

His Holiness smiled at her gently before looking over at me. And I knew in that moment that he recognized what had been revealed that afternoon.

"When we keep our guru in our heart," he looked back at Zahra, in confirmation. "We will always be safe."

"Even if we fall asleep in a laundry basket?" queried Oliver.

They all burst out laughing.

After they had gone, and Oliver had collected up various documents and left too, the Dalai Lama made his way from his desk to an armchair near the windowsill. There he sat, resting for a few moments, just him and me in the deepening twilight.

I thought how much of the time I was in the presence of His Holiness he was alone and in silence. And how, in the many hours we spent together this way, I had never once had the sense of inactivity. Of absence. Of nothing happening.

On the contrary. I had always known that, just as he began each day with five hours of meditation, his work in the world arose from stillness. His actions might appear spontaneous and without effort, penetrating the hearts and minds of many beings continuously and without ceasing. But it all came from this place, here. From the tranquil presence that was the ground of all possibilities.

It was a knowingness that I sensed would never end; too many of us depended on him still. Unlike a Buddha, we were beings with needs.

As I shared the stillness, I did so in the light of the afternoon's revelations, with a sense of belonging. A heartfelt reassurance of where I'd come from and of being in the right place. Of purpose and direction. Most of all, with a profound connection to the small group of fellow travelers with whom I had shared several lifetimes. It was a feeling of such delightful, pervasive contentment that I couldn't help but purr.

After a while, the Dalai Lama looked up at where I sat facing him on the windowsill.

"It is said that each one of us has been a mother to every other living being, at some time in the past," he gazed at me with open-hearted benevolence. "Imagine, little Snow Lion, if we could all feel that connection, as if it were real?"

EPILOGUE

DO YOU EVER GET THE FEELING THAT LIFE COASTS BY FOR LONG stretches of time, during which nothing much of any consequence happens. Then suddenly, without warning, there's a burst of activity—and all sorts of game-changing events occur which seem to shift your world on its axis?

That's how it seems to me, dear reader. And it certainly felt like that on a particular day down at The Himalaya Book Café where I'd gone for lunch. Head Waiter Kusali, looking particularly dapper in a brand new uniform, presented me with some of the tastiest morsels of that lunchtime's *sole meunière*, which I ate with great relish. Then I climbed to the top shelf of the magazine rack, washed my face, and lay down for a post-lunch siesta.

So far, so normal—just another day in the rarefied existence of His Holiness' Cat.

But was it my feline sixth sense or simple coincidence that made me stir from my slumbers and open my eyes at the precise moment four men in dark suits and sunglasses arrived at the front door? The appearance of suited men wasn't in itself unusual. But the men had an air of secrecy and importance about them, as they made their way to the back of the café with purposeful discretion.

Within moments, Kusali was conferring with them, head tilted towards theirs in a guarded manner. Then he was nodding across the room to Franc, who immediately crossed the room to join them. As he did, I noted a flash of excitement in his eye; it seemed to me that theirs was a visit he had been expecting.

After the briefest of conversations, Kusali and Franc showed the men, not to a table, but to everywhere but. One suited fellow made his way into the kitchen. Another went up the stairs and poked about in Serena's office. A third began prowling through the shelves of the bookstore, while the fourth snooped around the restaurant surreptitiously, looking here and there for who knew what.

At that exact moment, Serena arrived through the front door, in time to take over the café management. Noticing a suited stranger checking behind the restaurant curtains, before spotting another one bending behind one of the bookshelves, as soon as she caught sight of Franc she raised her eyebrows,

"What's with?" She tilted her head in the direction of the man behind her.

"Special Protection Group." When her expression didn't change, he continued, "They look after government ministers. That kind of thing."

"But why here?" She raised her hands.

"Security clearance. Seems that we're expecting some kind of VIP."

Serena glanced around the restaurant. It was the mid-afternoon lull, so few of the tables were occupied. "How many are we expecting? Have they made a booking?" she asked.

Franc raised a hand to the side of his face. "I think it's to do with you," he told her. Then shrugging, "I don't know how many. They said something about a community award."

"That!" She pulled a face, before pausing. "That was weeks ago. Anyway, I told them to send me whatever by post."

"Seems like someone's coming here anyway to present it to you."

Serena glanced at the reflection of herself in the glass pane of the manager's office, eyebrows furrowing. "Did they say who and when?"

"Some minister," Franc was vague. "In an hour's time."

She was shaking her head. "I'm really not dressed for … officialdom. My shift starts in less than five minutes."

"I'm not going anywhere," Franc was adamant. "As if I'm leaving here when some VIP from Delhi is about to arrive! Go home and change, if you like. I'll take care of the shop."

Serena regarded him closely. "Only if you don't mind," she said.

"Just go," he pointed to the door. "We'll be here for you when you get back."

Serena about turned, heading quickly in the direction from which she'd come. Watching her retreating figure, Kusali sidled up to Franc.

"Shall I prepare the room?" he asked, always the master of discretion.

"Please," Franc confirmed, drawing a phone out of his pocket. "I'll send the group text."

Within a short while, every single one of the café's waiting staff—both those on shift as well as others who had been summoned—were rearranging the whole restaurant. They carried tables to the side to clear a large space. They installed a platform, consisting of wooden pallets which had been lying out the back of the restaurant for some weeks, topped with sturdy hardwood panels. They draped bunting behind the dais and around the walls, as well as on the awnings outside the café.

Sam set up a microphone and speakers. Angela decorated the place with large framed photographs on easels, showing groups of Indian teenagers studying at computers; holding graduation certificates; and smiling broadly outside workplaces having secured their first job. They were images Serena used to have for inspiration on her computer screen upstairs. For the first time, they were being put on public display.

Bronnie was the first guest to arrive, sometime later. By now, the room was all set for a VIP visit, Kusali presiding over a few finishing touches with his usual aura of effortless command.

Sam came out to see Bronnie, at which point Ewing Klipspringer arrived, making his way towards the two of them in his trademark tennis shoes.

"All decked out for the big night," Ewing glanced around the place admiringly.

"Are you going to play some piano for us tonight?" Bronnie nodded towards the upright in the corner, where Ewing sometimes performed.

"If I'm called upon—certainly," he clasped his hands, cracking his knuckles theatrically. "But tell me about you guys. Are you still living in the hell realms, next to the woman with smoked fish and violent rages?"

Bronnie was shaking her head.

"Same apartment," replied Sam. "But things moved on in the strangest of ways."

"They did?" Ewing looked intrigued.

"Turns out that the whole thing was caused by a lock on Mrs. William's kitchen door. It was too high for her to reach. So when she cooked kippers, there was no ventilation and the smoke went straight up into our apartment."

"And when she did open the door, like a couple of days a week," Bronnie took over, "she had her son, Barry, come over to lock up. He'd stay for dinner and they'd drink too much and before you knew it, they'd be at it ..." Bronnie was shaking her head.

"So, you got her to change the lock?" queried Ewing.

"**That** wasn't going to happen," Sam spoke with conviction. "But when we phoned the rental agent and told him we'd pay to have it changed, a locksmith was out the next day."

"Problem solved?" smiled Ewing.

"There was all the stuff in the hallway," said Bronnie. "But we're clearing it out, bit by bit."

"And the final showdown before the son left for England." Sam rolled his eyes.

Ewing looked from one to the other. "But what an amazing turnaround."

"It would never have happened if Sam hadn't delivered some flowers to her in hospital, after a fall," Bronnie slipped her arm around him, appreciatively.

"And that would never have happened," Sam was quick to point out, "but for Geshe Wangpo's advice."

"He told you to take her flowers?"

"Not directly," replied Sam.

"What he said," said Bronnie, "was that trying to be a bodhisattva doesn't make you a doormat. Along with compassion, we need wisdom and power. We didn't have any power in that situation. But when she had a fall and flowers arrived from a friend, then we heard she was in hospital. Then we had some power, so we used it."

"We tried to think of her as our Precious Treasure," Sam told him.

"Ah yes. Geshe Wangpo's Precious Treasures," Ewing chuckled. "I have a few of those myself!"

More people were arriving at the café, unusually formal in dresses, jackets and even a few ties. There were friends of Serena's from her childhood days, like the Cartright family. Others who knew her through Sid or from her work on the spice pack business. A group of young Indian men in dark pants and white shirts appeared and soon gathered around the framed photos Angela had displayed; evidently they were some of those who had benefited from the upskilling program.

Kusali directed waiting staff, who appeared from the kitchen in immaculate starched white uniforms, carrying trays of tinkling drinks. Franc, freshly changed into a tasteful jacket and tie, stood at the door of the café, warmly greeting his guests.

The four dark-suited men from the Special Protection Group had, I observed, been joined by colleagues and had stationed themselves at all the entrances to the room, as well as strategic spots outside, where they muttered to each other using microphones concealed in their suit sleeves.

When Conrad walked through the door, it took me a few moments to recognize him. Not only on account of his stylish jacket and tie, but also because of his relaxed demeanor. Stepping into the café, he glanced around with nonchalant ease before spotting Angela, who had joined Sam, Bronnie, Ewing and some of the other yoga school people near the magazine rack.

Angela, who had changed into an elegant, emerald-green dress, hugged him appreciatively.

"So handsome!" she beamed.

"And look at you!" he gazed at her with a twinkle.

"Young love!" Ewing regarded them indulgently.

"You've certainly come out of your shell," Merrilee, never backward in coming forward, waggled a finger at him. "I thought you were the strong, silent type," she accused him in her gravelly voice.

"Silent perhaps," he shrugged. Then as they laughed, "And I took myself far too seriously. I have only recently come to understand," he leaned forward, about to communicate a wisdom of great importance, "there is no self to take—seriously or otherwise."

"The great ghost of the self," confirmed Sam.

"The cause of so much pain," agreed Ewing.

A waiter arrived bearing a tray laden with flutes of champagne and sparkling water. Knowing Merrilee of old, he proffered the tray in her direction first. "A drink, ma'am?" he asked.

Merrilee, who had been in The Himalaya Book Café all of five minutes gave him a look of faux anxiety. "I thought you were never coming!" she said, helping herself to a glass of bubbly.

Guests continued to stream in, and the top shelf of the magazine rack was the perfect vantage from which to watch events unfold. While some of the arrivals were regulars at the café, many of them were not. I was surprised, however, when in through the door stepped none other than Tenzin and Oliver.

Being familiar with The Downward Dog School of Yoga, on account of Ludo's long association with the Dalai Lama, they came over to join the yoga group.

Tenzin glanced about the room, "Quite a turnout!"

"The Who's Who of Dharamshala," confirmed Ewing in a gently ironic tone.

"And not just the human variety," said Oliver drolly, nodding in my direction.

"It's amazing they've managed to keep this whole thing under wraps from Serena," said Ewing.

"She has no idea?" asked Tenzin.

"None whatsoever," he gestured over to where Franc was shaking hands at the door. "Franc sent her home to get changed half an hour ago. She thinks there's some government bureaucrat coming in with a certificate. Sid will make sure they stay home until he gets the all clear. He and Franc have been working on this for weeks."

"Are we expecting Ludo this evening?" asked Tenzin, after looking around.

Ewing shrugged.

"He's expected back this week," said Suki. "No-one seems to know exactly when."

Moments later, a woman was tapping Oliver on the arm and engaging him in conversation. There was something familiar about her face, but dressed formally, with elegantly coiffed dark hair, I couldn't place her. She seemed to have something in particular she wanted to tell him, leading him away from the yoga group in the direction of the magazine rack.

"It really was the most unusual turn of events," she was telling Oliver as they drew closer.

Oliver's eyes flashed expectantly behind his glasses.

"We fare welled one of our residents last week," she said, with a meaningful expression.

"I'm sorry."

"In our line of work …" she shrugged. "Hilda had been ill for a long time. Towards the end she was dependent on breathing tubes, poor love. Not much quality of life."

Oliver nodded.

"In her final days, one of the few things that gave her joy was our new visitor, the Therapy Cat."

"Oh, yes?" Oliver was amused.

"I think I mentioned to you before how good the cat is with our residents. And you told me she sounded like the Dalai

Lama's Cat."

Oliver was nodding. "She fitted your description."

"Anyway, I told the lady and her daughter about the identity of the cat. They were absolutely thrilled! It was as though they were receiving the blessings of the Dalai Lama himself. That was the day before the old lady died."

Oliver looked as though he was about to say something. But the woman, who I now knew to be Marianne Ponter, manager of the nursing home, held up her hand. "That's not the end of it."

"No?"

"Hilda was on her own when she died. Early in the evening. Her daughter had gone home to make dinner for her husband, who was back from six weeks at sea—he's a ship's captain. It's often the way, you know. They hold on till their loved ones have the emotional support they need, then as soon as that happens, they slip away."

Oliver was following her intently.

"Anyway, the daughter came back that evening, and we had to break the sad news, which we'd only just discovered ourselves. She wanted to see her mother one last time, and that's when we took her through to the room to find this." Unclasping the handbag strapped around her right arm, the woman drew out a small, transparent, zip-sealed plastic bag, containing several generous tufts of cream-colored fur. She handed the bag to Oliver.

"It seems that our Therapy Cat is more than that. The evidence is that she was with our resident right at the very end."

Nodding contemplatively, Oliver said, "*Anam Cara* is the Celtic expression."

"*Anam Cara?*" Marianne repeated.

"Translates as "soul friend". An Anam Cara may play the role of death midwife, helping a being through an important time of transition."

"Well, she gave our resident joy in her last days and, we suspect, helped her through a peaceful death. The lady's daughter was so very grateful. And she made me take this fur—strictly on loan—to check if it was, in fact, the Dalai Lama's Cat who came visiting. For her that would be ..." she bit her lip to stem her own, rising emotion as she shook her head, "more than wonderful."

"I'm pretty sure this is her. But you don't need me to confirm." Oliver handed her back the bag. "If you turn round right now, you'll find that she's sitting beside you."

"Good heavens!" Marianne exclaimed, turning to look at me.

As I'd been sitting in the same position for quite some time, I flopped onto my side and stretched out across the full width of the rack, my front paws quivering out towards the two of them. I held her gaze with an expression of clear-blue lucidity.

"Oh yes," she said appreciatively, reaching out to stroke me. "Without a doubt. This is our visitor."

"She gets around, don't you HHC?" said Oliver.

"What did you call her?"

"HHC. His Holiness' Cat. She is a feline of many names and titles. And as you have just confirmed, whenever something of particular importance happens around here, HHC is mysteriously there to witness it."

"Omniscient?" Marianne queried, turning back to meet my sapphire-blue scrutiny.

"Good as," chuckled Oliver.

As if to prove his point, at that moment, with the café filled to capacity, there were gestures towards the door and people turned as Serena, hand in hand with both Zahra and Sid, appeared round the corner, making their way to the entrance of The Himalaya Book Café. Serena was radiant in a coral-colored dress and sparkling jewelry, dark hair flowing down to her waist. Sid was formally attired in his Maharajah robes, the turban on his head decorated with a bejeweled spray of feathers. Zahra, in a turquoise dress, was wearing make-up that made her look very grown-up—and a tiara that twinkled on her head.

Serena was first to see the bunting that now decorated the café awnings, then all the people inside wearing suits and dresses. She turned to Sid, wagging her finger in mock indignation. Franc was at the front door to meet them, and she was evidently accusing the two men of being in cahoots—as indeed they had been—before, with a roll of the eyes, she accepted the situation, and warmly greeted the guests nearest the door.

Besieged from all sides, Serena and Sid had been caught up near the entrance for some time, when one of the Special Protection Group tapped Franc on the shoulder and gestured towards his watch. Franc quickly shepherded Serena, Sid and Zahra towards the temporary stage that had been put up along the side of the café.

From snatches of conversation about the room, it was clear that no-one had any idea who would be arriving to present Serena with her award. As Serena, Sid, Zahra and Franc stood on the dais, and a conversational lull fell across the room, there was an air of intrigue and anticipation.

Suddenly, Serena pointed outside as a taxi pulled up. From out of the back climbed Ludo in a white, linen suit, soon followed by a beautiful young woman in an emerald evening dress. Looking every bit his usual poised self, Ludo placed a proprietorial hand on the waist of the woman and guided her to the café door.

"Welcome home!" Franc greeted them, using the stage microphone. "You're just in time!"

Seeing Serena and Sid on stage in their finery, Ludo made a show of folding his hands at his heart and bowing towards them, which they reciprocated, amid warm laughter. Proceeding down the narrow aisle that had formed between front door and stage, Ludo turned to all and announced in that distinctive, Germanic accent, "I look forward to introducing you all to this beautiful young lady, Heidi. She is a wonderful yoga teacher, who also happens to be my niece!"

There was a round of applause and Sid, Serena and Zahra bent down to exchange greetings with the late arrivals, who apparently had arrived home less than an hour earlier.

There was a commotion outside as motorbike outriders roared past slowly, followed by several police cars, then two very long, black executive limousines, hoods mounted with the Indian flag. A flurry of Special Protection Group officers surrounded the first of these. As it came to a slow halt, they opened the rear door directly outside the front of The Himalaya Book Café. Anticipation inside the café had mounted dramatically, with the appearance of the cavalcade as well as the show of security. The guests had arrived expecting some anonymous government official to present Serena with an award, but the stakes had suddenly and dramatically risen.

It seemed an age before there was any movement from the back seat of the car. Armed security men were fanning out around the vehicle, surveying the street and rooftops, gesticulating urgently to one another. Only after an all clear had been given, two sandaled feet appeared, followed by legs in white churidar pants, then a cream Nehru jacket.

The figure emerging from the car was none other than the Prime Minister of India.

There was a collective gasp of surprise—not least on the part of Serena—followed by an awed hush. The Prime Minister made his way through the doors of the café, greeting all present by bringing his palms to his chest, and nodding from one side to the other as bodyguards ushered him to the stage. Franc introduced him to Serena, Sid and Zahra, before taking to the microphone and formally announcing, "Most honored guests, ladies and gentlemen. I am delighted to welcome to The Himalaya Book Café, the leader of the world's largest democracy, the Prime Minister of India!"

The Prime Minister responded to the thunderous applause with a delighted smile, before gesturing for quiet. "I know you didn't want a fuss to be made," he began, looking at Serena and prompting laughter. "So I promise not to stay long. As it happens, I'm on my way to visit one of India's most honored guests up the road."

As he pointed to the front door, he noticed that somehow, in the flurry between his arrival and this moment, the honored guest he was referring to had made his own, quiet appearance. At the front door, the Dalai Lama was standing between two of his own very large bodyguards.

The Prime Minister immediately gestured that His Holiness should join him. Moments later, the Dalai Lama was making his way to the stage too. On reaching it, he stood near the end of the line-up, taking Zahra's hand in own right hand and Franc's in his left.

Am I making too much of this, dear reader, or was it the case that, as he surveyed all present with his distinctive smile, he paused for a meaningful moment, glancing from Zahra towards me?

"A certificate could certainly have been put in the post," continued the Prime Minister, after greeting His Holiness warmly. "But it is important to me that I don't lose touch with people. And of course, it is especially important to pay tribute to those who work quietly behind the scenes to achieve extraordinary results. We are all familiar with names like Mother Teresa. However it is not name or fame but what you bring to your work that is important, wouldn't you agree, Your Holiness?"

The Dalai Lama nodded. "Intention," he agreed.

"There are many with good intentions to help others in need," continued the Prime Minister. "In our busy world, it can be hard to follow up such intentions with meaningful actions. Serena," he paused for emphasis, turning to look at her, "you are one such person. A child of India, you moved to Europe as a young adult and were very successful in your career."

Serena glanced down, modestly.

"You could have stayed there. But you returned, and when you did, you saw a need that you were able to do something about."

The Prime Minister went on to tell his audience about the hundreds of teenagers who learnt computer skills each year, thanks to sponsorship from Serena's spice pack business. The thousands who had, in the past five years, found jobs. And the tens of thousands of lives that had been freed from the unrelenting grind of poverty.

While most people in the café were aware that Serena spent part of each day in the office upstairs managing her business, few knew about the scale of her operation—or the very many lives she had touched. Deepening this recognition was the fact that the Prime Minister of India himself was in their midst, having gone out of his way to thank her for her contribution.

As everyone looked at Serena with renewed respect and appreciation, the Prime Minister gestured to three of the young people who had arrived earlier. Somewhat nervously, they joined the group on stage.

After a reassuring nod from the Prime Minister, and a quick hug from Serena, a studious and bespectacled young man named Rohan briefly explained how he had been living in difficult circumstances with relatives in Dharamshala, until the opportunity to learn computer skills had come up. After the course, he had quickly found work with a phone company, and now supported both himself and his relatives. Although apprehensive about being thrust into the limelight, the quiet pride with which he spoke of the turnaround in his life wasn't missed by anyone.

Beaming Sahil won everyone over with his high voltage smile. Having previously searched for food in garbage bins outside restaurants, he now worked in a big hotel where, he explained excitedly, he planned to become managing director one day.

Then it was Aasha, the young woman holding the hand of her three-year-old daughter who touched everyone deeply, as she recounted losing both her husband and home because of a railway accident. It was only the training and help from Serena to find work that had saved her from the streets.

There wasn't a dry eye in the room by the end of Aasha's testimony. And no words for the profound emotions evoked by the three young people, who left the stage to a round of spontaneous and heartfelt applause. The recognition was growing of just how extraordinary Serena's work had been. And then the Prime Minister announced that, as well as a certificate, he had brought with him a Community Service Medal to present to her.

Evidently well-versed in the theatrics of the occasion, and watched by everyone closely, he drew from his pocket a gold-colored medal on the end of a multi-colored ribbon. "On behalf of the Republic of India," he announced, stepping forward towards Serena, "I endow you with this medal in grateful recognition for your very significant contribution to the health and happiness of our people."

Serena bowed her head as the Prime Minister placed the ribbon around her neck. Looking up, her eyes glistened with tears. Sid stepped over to hug her, and the whole place erupted in hand clapping and roars of approval. Mrs. Trinci was not to be stopped from clambering onto the stage to hug her daughter effusively—and then almost smothering the Prime Minister. One of Serena's former students came to the stage to present her with a huge bouquet of flowers, as Franc gave her a hug. All the while, the Dalai Lama watched events unfold, smiling, applauding and absorbing not only Serena, but everyone else in the room with his presence of heartfelt benevolence.

Freed from Mrs. Trinci's embrace and on the point of leaving, the Prime Minister turned to His Holiness and asked if he would like to say anything. The Dalai Lama was thoughtful for a moment. Then, stepping to the microphone, he took Serena's hand in his. "I have known Serena since she was a little girl, he was nodding. "And always, she has had a good heart. Helping others. Practicing kindness. This is what's important, no?"

As happened so often when His Holiness spoke, everyone in the room was totally absorbed in what he was saying. And in that moment, what he was saying made overwhelming and self-evident sense.

"Official recognition," he smiled at the Prime Minister. "This is very nice. Wonderful! But the true reward," he was touching his heart, "it is here." Turning to Serena he asked,

"You feel it?"

Serena, biting her lower lip to hold her composure, nodded.

The Dalai Lama squeezed her hand. "This is only the beginning," he said, enigmatically. "There are very good things to come."

Moments later, His Holiness and the Prime Minister were being escorted out of the room by their security teams to the waiting vehicles. Sid and Zahra huddled with Serena and Franc briefly, before Franc took to the microphone.

"Our waiting staff members are about to bring out food and drinks, and I welcome you all to stay with us to celebrate. But," he held up his hand imperatively, "I want you to stay right where you are for just a moment."

Turning, he gestured to where Serena had slipped her left arm around Sid's waist and her right around Zahra's. Smiling broadly, and looking unusually self-conscious, she nodded from one to the other as the three stepped forward to the microphone.

"Just one other announcement of a more personal nature," she glanced about the room where all her family members, friends and colleagues were gathered. "I'm pregnant!"

The whoops of excitement and applause that followed were of a different nature to those that had accompanied her recognition by the Prime Minister. Everyone in the room wanted the very best for Serena, and knew how much this meant to her and Sid. Zahra, too, looked delighted that she would soon be greeting a baby brother or sister into the world.

Coming down from the stage, the three of them were mobbed by friends and loved ones, just as Kusali directed his waiters to fan through the room, their trays loaded with champagne. In a moment of impulsive excitement, Ewing Klipspringer sat down at the piano and launched into an upbeat medley. As glasses clinked, congratulations were shouted, and dozens of excited conversations blossomed—and the noise level rose by many decibels. The top shelf of the magazine rack was no longer a congenial spot for a cat.

Not that I had to wait long. No sooner had my thoughts turned to escape than Zahra appeared. Lifting me from the shelf, she held me to her chest and headed for the front door, where I thought she would put me down.

Instead, she walked on out. Away from the noisy celebrations at the café and up the road towards Namgyal. "Don't worry, Rinpoche, I'll get you home safely," she promised, walking swiftly on. "I know you wouldn't want to be stuck back there."

I nuzzled into the curve of her neck. And as we continued towards Namgyal in the late afternoon, a cool breeze blowing up the Kangra Valley from the Himalayas, I mused how a lifetime ago, Zahra and I had almost certainly found ourselves in much the same situation—only in reverse. The revelations we had experienced several days ago at the feet of Yogi Tarchin had been quite extraordinary and, as I was discovering, they continued to bring a special poignancy to most everyday encounters, such as this one. It was as if the meeting and parting over lifetimes, the heartfelt resonance of connection we had always felt—and now better understood—transformed even mundane encounters into moments of inestimable value.

She carried me through the gates of Namgyal and across the courtyard home. As we reached the entrance, she placed me gently on the pavers. Out of habit I checked the first-floor window, where I spent so much of my life surveying the comings and goings at the monastery and temple. As I did, I saw His Holiness looking down directly at the two of us.

I paused. Zahra followed my gaze, before bringing her palms together at her heart which the Dalai Lama reciprocated. As he held us in his gaze, I did not doubt for a moment that he knew exactly who we were, who we'd been, and the intricate web of connections that had held us together through the dance of many lifetimes.

When I walked into our room, the Dalai Lama was standing in the center of it, talking to Tenzin and Oliver. By the sound of it, they were planning the final details of the Prime Minister's imminent visit to Namgyal Monastery.

Having gone through logistics and timing, Oliver had one final question to raise. "On the matter of a parting gift, Your Holiness, would you like to suggest a book? Shantideva?"

The Dalai Lama pondered on this for a moment. "An Indian master? Good! But I'm not sure he will read it."

Tenzin suggested a few texts by Tibetan teachers. His Holiness remained unconvinced.

Oliver half turned to look at where I had taken up my usual occupancy on the sill. "We really do need that book, HHC."

"*The Four Paws of Spiritual Success*," nodded the Dalai Lama. "Yes, I would give him **that** book, without hesitation!"

Eventually, a gift book was agreed upon and the two Executive Assistants left the room, so that it was just His Holiness and me. He came over to the sill and sat beside me for a moment, the simple fact of his presence, in such close proximity, causing me to purr.

"Ah yes, my Snow Lion," murmured the Dalai Lama. "More than anything, **that** is the feeling I want you to communicate in your book. So that anyone who reads it feels that their life has been touched by loving kindness." He reached out to stroke me. "And also, wisdom. The four aspects of the path we are reminded about every time we see a Buddha."

As it happened, I was again looking directly at the wall-hanging of Shakyamuni Buddha as His Holiness spoke. Still searching for the four different aspects. But where were they?

After a few moments, His Holiness responded. "The lotus, symbol of renunciation."

Of course! For years I had known that lotus flowers, which rose from the mud of the swamps to exquisite beauty, were the symbol of renunciation. Without suffering, there was no motivation to seek transcendence. No mud, no lotus. But it was only now I realized that every single Buddha I'd ever seen in a painting or statue sat on a throne made from a lotus. The reminder had been there all along, hidden in plain sight!

"Next, the silver moon cushion, symbol of bodhicitta."

Again, I had taken for granted the radiant silvery-white cushion on which every Buddha sat or stood, never giving a moment's thought as to why it was there, or what it meant. But

I understood that the mind of enlightenment, bodhicitta, was often likened to moonlight, the impact of compassion having a calming, almost magical effect on the all those that it touched—just like the tranquil luminosity of the moon.

"The gold sun cushion, symbol of sunyata. Sometimes shown directly. If not, it is always implied."

Sunyata, I also knew, could be likened to the sun, because the dazzling radiance of wisdom eliminated the darkness of ignorance. Many Buddha images, like the one I was gazing at now, depicted only the silver cushion, with the gold one suggested by a ring of yellow.

"And finally the Buddha, the guru, symbol of the enlightened mind. When we bow to the Buddha or the guru, we do so not only out of reverence for him or her. We are also bowing to our own Buddha nature, our own capacity for enlightenment. This is the real reason. But you knew that, little Snow Lion, didn't you?"

My purring rose in appreciation. I had known about the images and their meaning for some years, but I had never put them together—until now. Glancing from the wall-hanging of Shakyamuni Buddha, to a beautiful statue of White Tara, to a painting of Buddha Manjushri, I could see it was the same for each one of them.

"Every Buddha is a visual reminder of the four elements of our spiritual journey," confirmed the Dalai Lama. "For those who don't understand their meaning, the symbols have no purpose. But for those of us who do—they are ever-present for us."

It was only because of His Holiness that I understood this. In truth, everything I knew that was of particular value was thanks to him. I may not be capable of the meditative concentration with which he began each day, the five hours of silence from which everything else arose. But **he** was capable of it. And from this open state he arose to benefit everyone he encountered, beginning with the luxuriantly furry being sitting right beside him.

Contemplating all that I had learnt in recent weeks, in particular the knowledge of how I was connected to those closest to my heart, I had never felt such profound appreciation. Nor had I ever purred so loudly! My gratitude to the Dalai Lama was one which couldn't be expressed in sound or sensation. But as I turned to look up at him, he responded by bowing to touch my forehead with his own.

We remained like that, head to head, for the longest time. So long that after a while I could no longer feel where my body ended and the Dalai Lama's began. Or, for that matter, where one formless mental continuum became entrained with another.

From a distance came the wail of sirens and the roar of motorbikes as outriders approached the monastery. In a while, I knew, one of us would return to being His Holiness and another to being His Holiness' Cat.

But right now, together in the twilight, there was only boundless peace.

A NOTE FROM HHC

IF YOU WOULD LIKE TO DEEPEN YOUR UNDERSTANDING OF SOME of the key themes in this book, I have some whisker-tingling news for you!

Go to David Michie's website, click the 'Free Stuff' button, and you can download my booklet of meditation instructions: *The Four Paws of Spiritual Success: Meditations.* There is no charge for this download, although you will be prompted for your email address to receive David's monthly articles on Buddhism, mindfulness, reconnecting to nature and related themes.

You will also find other resources under Free Stuff, including audio meditations and short stories.

Warning: Please be aware that meditation will transform you into a cat-magnet and, for that matter, of keen interest to any other being with fur or feathers with whom you share your home. In the room where you sit, please leave the door ajar, so that others may join in your peace.

WWW.DAVIDMICHIE.COM

For your enjoyment, we have enclosed an extract
from David Michie's international bestseller,

The Magician of Lhasa [BOOK ONE]

Don't miss the exciting sequel:
The Secret Mantra

BOOK TWO OF *The Magician of Lhasa*

COMING SOON!

Available wherever books are sold.

THE MAGICIAN OF LHASA

A novice monk. A quantum scientist.
An ancient secret.

DAVID MICHIE

THE MAGICIAN OF LHASA

CHAPTER ONE

Tenzin Dorje (pronounced Ten-zin Door-jay)

ZHENG-PO MONASTERY, TIBET

MARCH 1959

I AM ALONE IN THE SACRED STILLNESS OF THE TEMPLE, LIGHTING butter-lamps at the Buddha's feet, when I first realize that something is very wrong.

"Tenzin Dorje!" Startled, I turn to glimpse the spare frame of my teacher, silhouetted briefly at the far door. "My room. Immediately!"

For a moment I am faced with a dilemma. Making offerings to the Buddha is considered a special privilege—and as a sixteen year old novice monk I take this duty seriously. Not only is there a particular order in which the candles must be lit. Each new flame should be visualized as representing a precious gift—such as incense, music and flowers—to be offered for the sake of all living beings.

I know that nothing should prevent me from completing this important rite. But is obedience to my kind and holy teacher not more important? Besides, I can't remember the last time that Lama Tsering used the word "immediately." Nor can I remember a time when anyone shouted an order in the temple. Especially not Zheng-po's highest-ranking lama.

Even though I am only half way through lighting the candles, I quickly snuff out the taper. Bowing briefly to the Buddha, I hurry outside.

In the twilight, disruption is spreading through Zheng-po monastery like ripples from a stone thrown into a tranquil lake. Monks are knocking loudly on each other's doors. People are rushing across the courtyard with unusual haste. Villagers have gathered outside the Abbot's office and are talking in alarmed voices and gesturing down the valley.

Slipping into my sandals, I gather my robe above my knees and, abandoning the usual monastic code, break into a run.

Lama Tsering's room is at the furthermost end, across the courtyard and past almost all the monks' rooms, in the very last building. Even though his status would accord him a spacious and comfortable room directly overlooking the courtyard, he insists on living next to his novices in a small cell on the edge of Zheng-po.

When I get to the room, his door is thrown open and his floor, usually swept clean, is scattered with ropes and packages I've never seen. His lamp is turned to full flame, making him look even taller and more disproportionate than ever as his shadow leaps about the walls and ceiling with unfamiliar urgency.

I've no sooner got there than I turn to find Paldon Wangpo hurrying towards me. The pair of us are Lama Tsering's two novices but we have an even stronger karmic connection: Paldon Wangpo is my brother, two years older than me.

We knock on our teacher's door.

Lama Tsering beckons us inside, telling us to close the door behind us. Although the whole of Zheng-po is in turmoil, his face shows no sign of panic. Though there is no disguising the gravity of his expression.

"I only have time to tell you this once, so you must please listen carefully," he looks from one to the other of us with a seriousness we only see before an important examination.

"This is the day we have feared ever since the year of the Metal Tiger. Messengers have just arrived at the village with news that the Red Army has marched on Lhasa. His Holiness, the Dalai Lama, has been forced into exile. A division of the Red Army is traveling here, to Jangtang province. At this moment they are only half a day's travel from Zheng-po."

Paldon Wangpo and I can't resist exchanging glances. In just a few sentences, Lama Tsering had told us that everything about our world had been turned upside down. If His Holiness has been forced to flee from the Potala Palace, what hope is there for the rest of Tibet?

"We must assume that the Red Army is coming directly towards Zheng-po," Lama Tsering continues quickly. From outside we hear one of the women villagers wailing. "If they travel through the night, they could arrive by tomorrow morning. *Definitely*, they could get here within a day.

"In other parts of our country, the army is destroying monasteries, looting their treasures, burning their sacred texts, torturing and murdering the monks. There's little doubt they have the same intentions for Zheng-po. For this reason, the Abbot is asking us to evacuate."

"Evacuate?" I can't contain myself. "Why don't we stay and resist?"

"Tenzin Dorje I have shown you the map of our neighbor China," he explains. "For every soldier they have sent to Tibet, there are ten thousand more soldiers ready to take their place. Even if we wanted to, this is not a struggle we can win."

"But-"

Paldon Wangpo reaches out, putting his hand over my mouth.

"Fortunately, our Abbot and the senior lamas have been preparing for this possibility. Each of the monks has a choice: you can return to your village and continue to practice the Dharma in secret. Or you can join the senior lamas in exile."

He holds up his hand, gesturing we shouldn't yet reply. "Before you say you want to join us in exile, you must realize this is not some great adventure. Traveling to the border will be dangerous—the Red Army will shoot dead any monks trying to leave. Then we must try to cross the mountains on foot. For three weeks we will have to travel very long distances, living off only the food we can carry. We will have to endure much hardship and pain. Even if we finally arrive in India, we don't know if the government will allow us to stay, or will send us back over the border."

"But if we return to our villages and continue to wear our robes," interjects Paldon Wangpo, "the Chinese will find us anyway, and punish our families for keeping us."

Lama Tsering nods briefly.

"If we disrobe, we would be breaking our vows." Paldon Wangpo has always been a sharp debater. "Either way, we would lose you as our teacher."

"What you say is true," Lama Tsering agrees. "This is a difficult decision even for a lama, and you are novice monks. But it is important that you choose, and do so quickly. Whatever decision you make," he regards each of us in turn, "you will have my blessing."

From outside comes the pounding of feet as people hurry past. There can be no doubting the crisis we're facing.

"I am now an old man, seventy four years of age," Lama Tsering tell us, kneeling down to continue packing a leather bag which is lying on the floor. "If I had only myself to think about, I might go into hiding and take my chances with the Chinese-"

"No lama!" I exclaim.

Next to me, Paldon Wangpo looks sheepish. He has always been embarrassed by my impetuosity.

"But the Abbot has asked me to play an important part in the evacuation."

"I want to come with you." I can hold back no longer, no matter what Paldon Wangpo thinks.

"Perhaps you like me as a teacher," cautions Lama Tsering. "But as a fellow traveler it will be very different. You are both young and strong, but I may become a liability. What happens if I fall and hurt myself?"

"Then we will carry you across the mountains," I declare.

Beside me Paldon Wangpo is nodding.

Lama Tsering looks up at both of us, an intensity in his dark eyes I have seen only on rare occasions.

"Very well-" he tells us finally. "You can come. But there is one very important condition I have to tell you about."

Moments later we are leaving his room for our own, having promised to return very quickly. As I make my way through the turmoil in the corridor outside I can hardly believe the condition that Lama Tsering has just related. This is, without question, the worst day in the existence of Zheng-po, but paradoxically for me it is the day I have found my true purpose. My vocation. The reason I have been drawn to the Dharma.

Opening my door, I look around the small room that has been my world for the past ten years; the wooden meditation box, three feet square. The straw mattress on the baked earth floor. My change of robes, and toiletry bag—the two belongings we are allowed at Zheng-po.

Not only is it hard to believe that I will never again sit in this meditation box, never again sleep on this bed. It is even more incredible that I, Tenzin Dorje, a humble novice monk from village of Ling, have been accorded one of the rarest privileges of Zheng-po. More than that—one of the most important tasks of our entire lineage. Together with Paldon Wangpo, and under the guidance of my kind and holy teacher, we are to undertake the highest and most sacred mission of the evacuation. It means that our flight from Tibet will be much more important—and more dangerous. But for the first time ever I know, in my heart, that I have a special part to play.

My time has come.

Matt Lester

IMPERIAL SCIENCE INSTITUTE

LONDON

APRIL 2006

I'M SITTING IN THE CRAMPED CUBBY-HOLE THAT PASSES FOR MY office, late on an overcast Friday afternoon, when my whole world changes.

"Harry wants to see you in his office," Pauline Drake, tall, angular and not-to-be-messed with, appears around the door frame two feet away. She looks pointedly at the telephone, which I've taken off its cradle, before meeting my eyes with a look of droll disapproval. "Right away."

I glance over the paperwork strewn across my desk. It's the last Friday of the month, which means that all timesheets have to be in with Accounts by five. As Research Manager for Nanobot, it's my job to collate team activities, and I take pride in the fact that I've never missed a deadline.

But it's unusual for Harry to dispatch his formidable P.A. down from the third floor—and with such an absolute demand. I can't remember the phrase "right away" being used before.

Something must be up.

A short while later I'm getting out from behind my desk. It's not a straightforward maneuver. You have to rise from the chair at forty five degrees to avoid hitting the shelves directly above, before squeezing, one leg at a time, through the narrow gap between desk and filing cabinet. Then there's the walk along a rabbit's warren of corridors and up four flights of a narrow, wooden staircase with its unyielding aroma of industrial disinfectant and wet dog hair.

As I make my way across the open plan section of the third floor, I'm aware of being stared at and people whispering. When I make eye contact with a couple of the HR people they glance away, embarrassed.

Something's definitely up.

To get to the corner office, I first have to pass through the anteroom where Pauline has returned to work noiselessly at her computer. She nods towards Harry's door. Unusually it is open. Even more unusually, an unfamiliar hush has descended on his office, instead of the usual orchestral blast.

When I arrive, it's to find Harry standing, staring out the window at his less-than-impressive view over the tangled gray sprawl of railway lines converging on Kings Cross Station. Arms folded and strangely withdrawn, I get the impression he's been waiting specially for me.

As I appear he gestures, silently, to a chair across his desk.

Harry Saddler is the very model of the Mad Professor, with a few non-standard eccentricities thrown in for good measure. Mid-fifties, bespectacled, with a shock of spiky, gray hair, in his time he's been an award-winning researcher. More recent circumstances have also forced him to become an expert in the area of public-private partnerships. It was he who saved the centuries-old Institute—and all our jobs—by doing a deal with Acellerate, an LA based biotech incubator, just over a year ago.

"A short while ago I had a call from L.A. with the news I've been half-expecting for the past twelve months," he tells me, his expression unusually serious. "Acellerate have finished their review of our research projects. They like Nanobot," he brushes fallen cigarette ash off his lapel. "They *really* like Nanobot. So much that they want to move the whole kit and caboodle to California. And as the program originator and Research Manager, they want you there too."

The news takes me completely by surprise. Sure, there've been visitors from the States during the past year, and earnest talk of information exchange. But I never expected the deal with Acellerate to have such direct, personal impact. Or to be so sudden.

"They're moving very quickly on this," continues Harry. "They want you there in six weeks ideally. Definitely eight. Blakely is taking a personal interest in the program."

"Eight weeks?" I'm finding this overwhelming. "Why do I have to move to California at all? Can't they invest in what we're doing over here?"

Harry shakes his head in weary resignation. "You've seen the new shareholder structure," he says. "As much as Acellerate talk about respecting our independence, the reality is that they hold a controlling interest. They call the shots. They can strip what they like out of the institute and there's really not a lot we can do to stop them."

I'm not thinking about Acellerate. I'm wondering about my girlfriend, Isabella. She's more important to me than anything else in the world and after three years of working long and hard for Bertollini, the drinks manufacturer, she's just been promoted to Group Product Manager. The idea of her leaving her new job is a non-starter and there's no way I'm leaving her behind in London, no matter how great the interest of the legendary Bill Blakely.

Harry mistakes the cause of my concern. "If you look at what's happened to the other research programs Acellerate have taken to LA," he reassures me, "they've gone stratospheric." Pausing, he regards me more closely for a long while before querying in a low voice, "Isabella?"

"Exactly."

"Take her with you!"

"It's not that simple. She's just been promoted. And she's close to her family."

"A girl like her," Harry has met her at institute functions over the years, "she'll get a job like that in Los Angeles," he snaps his fingers. "And you'll be giving her family a good excuse to visit Disneyland."

As always, Harry is trying to keep focused on the positive. I understand, and I'm all the more appreciative because I know how hard this must be for him. Nanobot has always been one of his favorites. It was Harry who brought me into the institute when he discovered the subject of my Masters thesis. Harry who nurtured the program through its early stages. He and I enjoy a close relationship—more than my boss, he's also my

13

mentor and confidante. Now, just as the program's starting to get interesting, he's having it taken off him. What's more, who's to say it will end with Nanobot? It seems that Acellerate can cherry pick whatever they like from the institute and leave Harry with all the leftovers. Small wonder he's in no mood for the Three Tenors.

"You really must see this as the opportunity that it is," he tells me. "With Acellerate behind you, you can accelerate the program way beyond what we can afford here. You could get to prototype stage in two, three years instead of seven or eight. With positive early tests the sky really is the limit. You'll be working at the heart of nanotech development for one of the best-funded scientific institutes on earth. Plus you'll even be able to catch a sun tan. Think of this as a great adventure!"

His phone rings, and we hear Pauline answering it outside. Evidently Harry has told her we aren't to be disturbed—something he's never done before.

There's another pause before I finally say, "I guess whatever way you package it, I don't have much choice do I? I mean, Acellerate aren't going to leave the program in London just because my girlfriend has changed jobs. And if I walk away from it, that's the last seven years of my life down the tubes."

He doesn't answer me directly, which I take as confirmation. Instead he says, "Look at me, Matt. Fifty four years of age. A little battle-wearied, a little scarred. But I've had my fifteen minutes in the spotlight. If it was just about me, I wouldn't have bothered trying to find a new partnership for the institute last year. I'd have just taken my chances with Government funding and hoped for the best."

I swallow. Harry has never spoken so directly to me before and I find his modesty humbling.

"But the Institute's not just about my ego or anyone else's. It's about the work we do. The science. All our research programs have the potential to transform peoples' lives. And of all the programs we're running," he regards me significantly, "*yours* is the most likely to make the most revolutionary impact."

I regard him closely.

"You're the first cab off the rank, Matt. It's flattering that Acellerate are so keen to take you off us. You're thirty four years old and this kind of opportunity doesn't come along often."

"It's a bit sudden, that's all," I'm nodding. "I mean, ten minutes ago, my main concern was getting the time sheets in."

Harry regards me with a look of benevolent expectation.

"I'm sure I'll get used to the idea."

"Good."

"I'll have to speak to Isabella."

"Of course." Harry reaches into a desk drawer, taking out a large white envelope which he hands me across the desk.

"Before you make up your mind, you might like to study the terms and conditions," he says.

A short while later I'm heading back to my office in a daze. Not only is Harry's announcement life-changing, the conditions of my appointment are way beyond anything I could have imagined. Almost too much to believe.

As I return through HR, I'm so preoccupied I don't notice anyone. Even the reek of the stairs passes me by. I'm trying to get my head around the paradox that this is terrible news for the Imperial Science Institute, but an amazing opportunity for me. That Isabella is almost certain to be upset by the same thing that is a personal endorsement beyond my wildest dreams. I hardly know what to make of it.

I return to the poky office which has been my home for the past seven years. The bulging shelves and worn metal filing cabinets. The tiny desk swamped with paperwork. It's hard to believe I might be about to leave this all behind. That I have, in my hands, an extraordinary offer that could change my life.

Our lives.

I have to speak to Isabella.

Chapter One of *The Magician of Lhasa* by David Michie, Copyright ©2017 Mosaic Reputation Management (Pty) Ltd, Australia.

Excerpt used with permission.

ABOUT THE AUTHOR

DAVID MICHIE IS THE AUTHOR OF A *THE DALAI LAMA'S CAT* series of novels, as well as non-fiction titles including *Buddhism for Pet Lovers*, *Why Mindfulness is Better than Chocolate*, *Hurry Up and Meditate* and *Buddhism for Busy People*. His books are available in 28 languages in over 40 countries.

In 2015 David founded Mindful Safaris, leading groups to Africa—where he was born and brought up— for journeys which combine game viewing with guided meditations. As the many returning members of the Mindful Safari family testify, these extraordinary experiences help us reconnect with nature, as well as with ourselves, in a relaxed yet powerful way.

WWW.DAVIDMICHIE.COM

CPSIA information can be obtained
at www.ICGtesting.com
Printed in the USA
LVHW022053121119
637080LV00005BA/697